Performance-Based Coaching

Performance-Based Coaching

Coaching

Move the Training Room Into the Classroom to
Accelerate Teacher Development

---

by Bradley Williams and
Kevin Clark

First Edition Printing

www.clarkconsultingandtraining.com

Performance – Based Coaching
by Bradley Williams and Kevin Clark
First Edition 2018

Library of Congress Cataloging-in-Publication Data

Clark Consulting and Training, Inc.
     Performance-Based Coaching™/ by Bradley Williams and Kevin Clark;
     illustrations by Bradley Williams and Kevin Clark
     p. cm.
     Includes bibliographical references and index.
     ISBN 978-0-692-19989-3
     LB 2018

Request for such permissions should be addressed:

Clark Consulting and Training, Inc.
16772 W. Bell Road Ste 110-612
Surprise, AZ 85374 – 9702
(623) 236 – 8376

Publishing Company:
Ingram Spark
www.ingramspark.com

Book Design:
W.K. Doggington, Intelligent Design Associates, L.L.C.
Cover Design:
P.H. Spousen, Forever Designs, Inc.
Printed in the United States of America

Contents

To the educational leaders who know - and have known -
that the time is now.

Introduction
Performance-Based Coaching

Welcome! You have probably picked up this book due to one of several predictable, yet sometimes discouraging, realities.

1. You are a district administrator who has worked to create strategic plan after strategic plan in an attempt to increase academic achievement for all learners in your district, only to find that implementation across various sites is inconsistent and that test results show wide variances among grade levels and teachers. Positive results are rarely sustainable.

2. You are a site leader who has been charged with supporting a district program only to find that your teachers struggle to connect this newest initiative to their past practices. Your exhortations to "get on board" are often met with an overwhelming resistance rooted in a culture that believes that *this too shall pass.*

3. You are an instructional coach who feels caught up in a low-intensity cycle of trainings, demonstration lessons and pre- and post-conferences. Your job is fragmented, and on a daily basis, most of your work seems stop-gap in nature and random in design. Many of the teachers you have worked with have either plateaued in their practice, asked to be released from your assistance, or put up roadblocks that hinder your effectiveness. You sometimes feel alone in your efforts to help teachers to improve.

While these scenarios seem almost tragic, they are alive and well at most schools and in most districts. The underlying reality is that typical approaches to teacher improvement — and hence educational improvement — represent a sad paradox: It is generally accepted that changes in teacher practices are needed to improve student learning and achievement. But no one wants to be the one who must change. Much like healthy eating, regular exercise and teeth flossing, most agree they are good practices – for someone else first. Add in local, state and national educational mandates that ask teachers to adopt or to discontinue practices that are one day "research based" and the next day on the scrap heap, and we have a toxic brew. For extra seasoning, stir in a portion of quick-fix hot tips and neat ideas from internet sources, then add some fun strategies from a couple of drive-by trainings and the recipe is nearly complete. The logical outcome is that most educators focus more on daily survival and justification of their current practices than on beginning and sustaining the hard work necessary to make lasting changes in their assumptions, beliefs and practices.

So why are traditional teacher development programs not working as intended to improve student achievement? And why do they consistently fail to transform school cultures or build sustainable systems? These questions —if taken seriously — forces us to confront another uncomfortable outcome. Study after study shows, similar to the experiences of most teachers, that most of what is learned in "training" is rarely implemented correctly, consistently, or with widespread enthusiasm. The result is an instructional program characterized not by what is common across grades and teachers, but by the huge differences in practice, both in terms of what is taught, how it is taught, and whether or not it is taught well. Visit four classrooms — or more if you can take it — on any site. It's a veritable free-for-all out there.

The glaring gap between what teachers learn in the training room and what gets implemented properly, effectively and sustainably in the classroom is the catalyst for this book and for our work as consultants and teacher educators. It is this *implementation gap* that is the true failure of our historical approaches to teacher development, school improvement and better student learning. That staff developers, school and district leaders, university academics and board members continue to endorse these failed approaches is testimonial to how resistant these parochial views are to change. But a new view and approach to teacher development is possible and is already taken hold in innovative schools and districts across the country.

This book lays out a comprehensive description, analysis, framework and steps for a far more effective theory and practice of how to help teachers to change in ways that benefit students. By understanding and implementing the information in this book, schools and districts have been transformed by a new energy for teacher learning, system-wide performance increases and innovation.

A key parochial assumption we tackle early in this book is that teachers are somehow different than any other professionals with respect to their learning. For decades, it was believed that teachers get all the learning and practice they need through their college or university preparation and teacher credentialing programs. Once in their own classrooms, the traditional model essentially says that change is now optional and left up to the individual teacher's discretion. Those "options" to change are provided typically through sit-and-get training sessions that focus mostly on one or the other end of the extremes: all theory and no practice, or rote implementation with no theory. Teacher conferences frequently function as options smorgasbords, replete with long spreads of tasty tips, fun ideas and entrees that distill complex ideas into bite-size finger foods for immediate consumption. In both settings, teachers are then generally left to return to their classroom and try to make *it* work — usually by themselves as they see fit, or to the best of their memory.

This approach to teacher development is at best fallacious, and at worst injurious, to students and the entire educational complex. Completing the cycle of paradoxes, teachers typically spend more than 95 percent of their teaching careers in their classrooms working with students, while 95 percent of their professional development time takes place in rooms where no children are present. We would be hard pressed to find another field that sees professional development as an isolated and largely theoretical exercise that takes place away from the actual work setting and removes those who are to be served. By separating teacher learning from its context (the classroom), professional development for many teachers is seen as something divorced from their daily work, as an interruption, or as a chance to rest. At its most extreme, professional development is viewed as a waste of time. As one 20-year veteran middle school teacher remarked when informed that the first three days of the school year were slotted for teacher development: "I have more important things to do this time of year. Do I have to go?"

Here is the good news. In this book you will find the information, tools and practical applications for changing teacher behavior in a way that moves the training room into the classroom, where the focus is solely on the proper implementation of new knowledge, skills and behaviors. In fact, the entire thrust of this book is to help educators — teachers, administrators, coaches, board members, teacher trainers, and university faculty — to see clearly how a departure from traditional "teacher training" practices can radically and fundamentally improve instruction for students, speed up implementation timelines for new initiatives, and create sustainable teacher behaviors that improve instructional outcomes for students. This approach is also far more cost effective than traditional teacher training, a critical factor in today's educational landscape.

At a systems level, the predictable outcome of implementing the coaching model presented in this book is almost always a renewed learning climate on campuses, new energy from teachers — novice and veteran-alike — and most important, immediate changes in practice that improve learning for students. For board members and other fiscally concerned observers, this coaching model represents an investment that yields far more than a dollar returned for a dollar invested. Indeed, like compounding interest in a savings account, our coaching model leverages scarce professional development dollars far in excess of other approaches by minimizing or eliminating out-of-class time for teachers, substitute costs and other expenses usually concomitant to sit-in-a-room staff development.

For students — who are after all the focus of teaching and of teachers — the results of this coaching model are simple and powerful: more teachers who do more things more frequently with greater efficiency, which almost always equates to more and better learning.

The central theses of this book, stated in few words, are as follows.

1. Measurable changes in teacher behavior are the sole focus of teacher development;

2. The implementation gap results from lack of effective in-class, behavior-focused coaching;

3. Performance-Based Coaching™ is the most efficient way to quickly improve teacher practices that are sustainable over time.

With these three assertions, we have therefore contradicted the majority of the theory and practice of traditional teacher training efforts, which are based on the following:

1. Staff development takes place away from the classroom and from interaction with students;

2. More emphasis is placed on feeling good about the change or understanding its supporting "scientific" evidence than on actually doing new and more effective behaviors;

3. Non-existent or poorly conceptualized and executed in-classroom support that is rarely designed to actually change teacher behavior.

At no time do we underestimate the complexity and challenge of changing teacher behavior. Instead, we will explore at a deep level why people change – or resist change – and apply very different theories, methods and techniques for getting teachers to do what is needed for improved student learning. The coaching system we present, referred to as Performance-Based Coaching™, is independent of content area, grade level, current teacher skill or any other factor.   What our system *is* dependent on are skilled instructional coaches and committed school and district leaders who understand three fundamental areas that are essential for bringing about changes in teacher behavior.

➢ How humans process and implement change

➢ How systems, namely schools and districts, can be structured to either support or to reject change efforts

➢ How to use specific coaching interventions to change teacher behavior

During the past 30 years, teacher improvement has been made far too difficult for everyone involved.   Sadly, efforts to "develop" teachers have more often created teachers who are cynical, bored, or fed up with the latest innovation that they know will quickly fade into the background. Many teachers relate fear and insecurity about being asked to implement new skills and knowledge with little or no assistance. When offered, external support is presented or perceived as a *gotcha*, wherein the acceptance of help is seen as a sign of weakness or a general condemnation of one's competence.

Our work with thousands of teachers across the country over the past two decades reveals a startling reality that precipitated most of the research and development of Performance-Based Coaching™. It is a similar refrain heard from teachers everywhere, and one that underscores the need for a more enlightened approach.

Sylvia, a teacher for 18 years, sounds like many of the teachers we have interviewed and coached:

> *"In all of my years of teaching, I have sat in rooms for hundreds of hours where I was told what to do and what to know. I have*

even been shown videos of what it should look like with students from some other place. But no one ever came to my classroom to show me or to help me figure out how to do it with my students."

This book aims to change that.

Chapter 1
The Predicable Failure Of Most Staff Development Efforts

Introduction

This year, thousands of teachers will sit down in cafeterias, conference rooms or empty computer labs across the country for something typically called *training, staff development* or *in-service*. While the topics, locations, teachers, trainers and snacks will vary, the common assumptions about how and why teachers will learn to do something new, better or different are usually the same. For the most part, teachers will sit, listen, probably do some small-group activities, usually get some new materials, and then be sent back to their classrooms to ostensibly implement everything they "learned". In those days following the training, the only certainty is that the new learning will be implemented variably. Many teachers will continue to implement their preferred style of instruction as though the training session never occurred. Some will try out the information, as they interpreted it, with very different levels of success. Others will severely modify what they learned to suit their beliefs and preferences. Some may even disparage the information. But regardless of their success, failure or rejection of the information, the one common denominator is that they will go it alone.

Objectives

In this chapter you will learn:

1. Why traditional teacher development efforts are based on a fundamentally flawed model of human and organizational learning

2. Why this flawed model is repeated year after year with the same poor results

3. How rationalizations and excuses are used to justify ineffective past practices

4. Why the traditional model is tantalizingly tempting for policy makers and educators alike

5. That responsibility for change in this model is placed solely on the teacher to "heal thyself".

You've Probably Seen Or Heard This Before

Mrs. Brown is a fifth-year teacher at an elementary school with about 850 students in a suburb of Houston, Texas. She has taught fourth grade for four of her five years teaching and has decided it is a grade level that suits her patient, yet energetic style. She enjoys discussing things with her students' maturing minds and is confident enough in her abilities as a teacher that she has a high tolerance for letting instruction flow to where students' interests lie. She is well-liked among the fourth-grade teaching team and by her students, and she is regularly requested by parents. During her time at the school, she has had two different principals, though she rarely interacted with either of them beyond matters of logistics and schedules. Her first principal seemed to frequently be away from the campus and only rarely popped into her classroom for a quick visit, usually with some visitor she was never introduced to, nor knew about, prior to the visit. The second principal, now in her second year at the school, frequently talks about needed changes in public education, but offers few specifics. She informed the staff when she arrived that she would spend the first year of her assignment "just looking, listening and learning in order to build relationships and to understand the site's unique culture."

When asked to describe the structure and content of her professional development during her first five years of teaching, Mrs. Brown easily lists the various focus areas: a content-area reading program for intermediate grades, a new math series, a supplement to the social science curriculum, a character-building program for students, a new way of offering intervention services to low-achieving students, a daily physical education sequence for students and, most recently, a positive behavior intervention system to improve management and decrease office referrals. She is not sure of the origin of most of the efforts, but she recalls that a new superintendent is a proponent of positive behavioral systems, and a now-departed curriculum director had rallied for the content-area reading program. For each of the initiatives, Mrs. Brown recalls at least two or three days of seminar-style training followed by randomly scheduled teacher meetings at the school. Asked to evaluate her level of implementation of the content and skills presented at the trainings, Mrs. Brown is quick to respond.

As fourth-grade teachers, we could not understand the content-area reading trainings because they seemed designed for high school students and teachers. We decided as a team to postpone using it. We use some of the behavior strategies, but when the new superintendent wanted a change in classroom management, it took away many of the systems that have worked in our classrooms for years. We hardly have time for social science, but the posters are useful when we get to it. The intervention program changed our daily schedules and kids leave the room, so I really don't know what they're doing there. We do the character education program about once a week, but I'm not sure what to do when kids don't seem interested in learning the life skills. I really like the PE program and found the training really motivating because of the facts the trainer presented about kids not moving or running anymore. A lot of the teachers don't do the PE program, though, but our new principal said they could use it as a pilot until they felt more comfortable with it.

Recipe For A Typical Teacher Development Effort

It is sometimes useful to label the parts of any process to better understand their order, their logical connectivity, and their projected outcomes. Much like planning a vacation, a map of where to start, where to end, the landmarks to look for along the way and some description of the experiences desired can make any activity involving humans more worthwhile and fulfilling. So, let's use this vacation analogy to label, to look for logic, and to identify the expected outcomes from a traditional public education teacher improvement effort.

Step 1: You (teacher) need *this*

The *this*, let's call it X, is usually decided by someone outside of the teacher's immediate web of colleagues, or is someone higher up the chain. Sometimes the reason for X's appearance is attributed to "them" or "they", "the state", or "research". For example, "They want us to focus on inquiry now and forget about practicing computation skills," or, "Research says you have to teach kids to be good citizens."

Step 2: Because

Little time is spent on why *this* is needed nor how *it* is logically related or unrelated to what you or other teachers are currently doing.

Time is precious in schools and districts, so instead of explaining in detail and with care the past and present situation, we instead "jump" to the change. This is analogous to someone knocking on your door to inform you that your house color will need to be changed immediately or that you will now be practicing a new religion.

Step 3: Now we're starting

This is pretty simple. It has been decided that you will start X on this date. You will begin on this date, for this amount of time and continue until you are told to start doing Y (the next new initiative). At such time, you will likely discontinue doing X.

Step 4: Here's your training

Time, date and place is all teachers need to know. Show up and listen to someone — usually a consultant, vendor or other expert — share something new, different, mandated, useful, fun, research-based, revolutionary, nonsensical, contradictory or incomprehensible.

Step 5: Go implement

Now that you have attended the training, you are ready, willing and able to get started with X. Go!

Step 6: Disagreement, misunderstandings, uncertainty, rejection, failure

Now that you are alone in your classroom, thoughts of the training get fuzzy, ideas are blurred, clear steps for getting started are missing, and you have many questions that will determine if you will keep doing X or forget about *it*.

Step 7: Rinse and Repeat

We can see from the steps above that the fundamental assertions of traditional change programs for teachers can be summarized as follows:

Teachers will change without any understanding of why the change is necessary and they will do so immediately, as instructed, and with minimal or no post-training assistance. Finally, they will self-certify that they have mastered the innovation and are implementing it as required until told to stop doing it, or they will remain silent and either modify it or not do it at all.

Wow! That is a harsh summation of traditional (and current) teacher development efforts. Laid out like this reveals its lack of grounding in either solid theory or solid practice, as well as providing us with many portholes through which to view and understand why it rarely works as a method for changing individual or group behavior. On the upside, it does conform to a very linear and aesthetically beautiful assumption about human change, namely that humans (read: teachers) will do and not do things as they are told, when they are told, and how they are told. Perhaps we are being too harsh. After all, much work by many people goes into planning and executing these types of learning efforts. So, to be fair, let's look at this model through the lens of different players in an educational organization to see why the model has endured so long and why it still is seen — year after year — as having potential to change individuals and organizations.

Through Your Eyes Only

You may recall the Chinese fable about a group of blind mice trying to determine what animal was in their midst (remember? an elephant). Each mouse drew a different conclusion as to what animal it was based on the small part with which they were in contact. And so, it is with teacher learning programs, so let's meet the people involved and explore their well-intentioned roles. By looking at our traditional teacher development model through various sets of eyes, we can better understand how its predictable and repeated failure is not what is envisioned by anyone, nor is it the culmination of a vast conspiracy. It's just what has always been done by people in these positions. And now, the players in the traditional teacher development program production and what they think they are really doing and why they do it.

Player	Their Responsibility	Their Theory of Human Change	Their Actions
Board Members	To approve or reject ideas	We decide what is best for our teachers and students	Approve the idea and its funding
District-level Administrators	To find new ideas and recommend, endorse or ignore them	We know best what teachers need	Put the best face possible on the idea and require its implementation
Site Administrators	To manage the message and implementation provided by district	We are brokers and we get teachers to do what we were told to get them to do, to "buy in" to the effort	Help, hinder or ignore the implementation at their site
Teachers	To attend training, implement what is learned	This is what I am supposed to be doing	Try, succeed, fail, adopt, reject, question, give up
Parents	To applaud or criticize the idea, to hope it works for their child	Just do what is best for my child please	Look for observable signs of improvement by their child

As we can conclude from the table above, no singular group deliberately sabotages the teacher development effort. Indeed, each believes their separate and stand-alone role, theory of human change and actions will work – in linear fashion – with the other players to bring about improvements in teaching and learning. Over time, as happens to any of us who performs a similar task repeatedly, the perspective of each player becomes even narrower as we work repeatedly within our "box". When things go wrong, each player usually seeks to justify that it wasn't their link of the chain that was weak. "We got you the funding you said you needed," says the board member to the district administrator at the first sign of poor or variable teacher implementation results. "Well, this was the best idea (program, strategy, tablet, smart board, etc.) that was available," says the district administrator. "I've tried to help them, but my teachers are struggling because the program is tedious and difficult to understand," says the site administrator. "We tried something similar 10 years ago and it didn't work, and it doesn't work now either," says the teacher. "But I thought this was based on research and would work with all kids," says the parent. And so it goes.

Death But No Funeral

There usually comes a time in almost all teacher development programs where no one is sure what exactly happened to "that initiative". The once-ballyhooed math manipulative program just faded away. The save-the-world computer time students had to have dwindled to almost never. And the writing across the curriculum initiative is now utilized by only a few teachers, all of whom must carpool to work together to keep it alive. Where did these and all of those ideas, materials, programs, theories and hundreds of staff development hours go? They just faded away with no formal announcement of their death, no funeral and no eulogy. But when the issue of their fade-out is broached, and reasons are sought for their disintegration, here is a popular sample of what you might hear in the staff lounge, on your walk to the staff parking lot or at a school board meeting.

1. "We needed more money."

2. "We needed more time."

3. "We needed more training."

4. "There was no buy-in."

Not surprisingly, the comments above link directly to six of the most common assumptions that knowingly or unknowingly are likely to guide your school's or district's next teacher change initiative. By defining each of these assumptions, we can better understand how the best-intentioned teacher development efforts can actually torpedo what we most want, namely more teachers who can do more things better in their classrooms to help students to learn. Let's first define the word *assumption,* because assumptions play a big part in how traditional teacher training programs are designed, implemented and analyzed. An assumption is simply something that, based on our life experiences, we consider to be true. They are so true, in fact, that we rarely — if ever — stop to reconsider whether they really are fact or our own brand of fiction. And why would we? They have explained the world to us for many years.

The second part of defining this word is recognizing that our assumptions govern – or at least provide a framework for – most of our behaviors. For example, if I assume that most students are hard workers, I might assign regular homework and assume that it will be completed. By contrast, if a teacher assumes that students are lazy and unwilling to work, the assigning of homework seems silly. All of us have an infinite number of assumptions about everything from punctuality to cleanliness to the role of a husband or wife. These invisible screens are far more powerful than most of us ever realize. After all, why would I re-think an assumption that has gotten me this far?

Six Common Assumption Traps About Teacher Change

1. More materials

The assumption: If teachers had newer, prettier, more expensive, better, electronic or digital materials, then they will teach better. By similar logic, if I had newer, chrome-plated weights, I could lift more. There are buildings in every school and districts full of materials from some other time. But if we had more, teachers would change.

2. Mandates

The assumption: Humans change best when given a mandate to do so. While this may work adequately in the military or other command-control environments, most people do not respond well to this approach. But might it work with husbands, wives or your own kids? If only it were so.

3. Motivation

The assumption: Teachers will be motivated to change their thinking, their attitudes and their behaviors if we tell them to be motivated to do so. Try this to test the veracity of this assumption: go to the library (actual or electronic) and randomly select a book from the non-fiction section. Now, motivate yourself to read that book and develop a passion for the topic it covered. Most of us have a natural affinity for quantum physics, Eastern cooking or neural pathway biology, right?

4. Mono-vision

The assumption: If we could just get teachers to do *this*, everything will be great. This suggests that a single thing (factor, idea, strategy, tip) is enough to radically improve such a multi-faceted task like teaching and learning. If teachers would just use graphic organizers three times a day, then all students would be in the top 10 percent in reading. If teachers gave students more wait time, then all kids would be great at solving double-digit multiplication problems. Pushed to its extreme, if all teachers did X, then all of our teachers would be considered excellent.

5. More Cowbell

The assumption: More of anything in education is better and preferable to less of anything. Have you ever attended a professional development session that focused on eliminating methods, strategies, materials or ideas from your teaching repertoire or from your grade level or school as a whole? Probably not. We just keep adding and adding things, believing that improvement is a function of addition. Now we do 15 things in quick bursts poorly, rather than five things well with adequate time.

6. Monastic Learning

The assumption: Humans learn new behaviors best when left alone to figure them out. Here is a simple challenge. Think of something you do well that you learned to do by yourself, independent of any assistance from another person. Keep thinking.

We have covered a lot of ground in this chapter and done so in a way that you may have found to be brash or callous. But if you found yourself recalling to mind examples as you read, then our descriptions are not off base. The point in covering this material early in the book is to challenge what has become an entrenched way of doing things with respect to teacher education that simply does not work, if it ever did. At a time when educators and their institutions are simultaneously being critiqued more and asked to do more, we need a new way to unleash the intellect and skills of teachers dedicated to their profession. The old ways simply don't work.

Things To Ponder Or Discuss

1. Do you respond favorably to people in your life who demand that you make an immediate and permanent behavioral change? How do you typically react to such demands?

2. How important is it that people know and understand the rationale for an organizational or a personal change?

3. What sustained behavioral change have you made in your life that regularly involves assistance from one or more people?

4. In your experience, how successfully have you seen teachers adapt to using new materials that they were simply told to use?

5. Do teachers secretly resist mandated changes in order to survive professionally and personally?

The Coaches Corner

When the typical teacher-change approaches described in this chapter are in play, coaches are frequently caught in a turbulent crosswind. Coaches are not immune from any of the thoughts, reactions, strengths or insecurities of a teacher, yet they are frequently asked to "get on board" with an effort and to get others to "buy in". The result can be a change in the coach's role from helping people to improve behavior to being a collector of complaints, frustration and gossip. If a change for teachers is based on the practices and assumptions described in this chapter, it does not bode well for the consolidation and effectiveness of the coaching role. In our surveys of hundreds of coaches, we have found that up to half go back to classroom teaching after just one year in the coaching role. Why? Most state that they were asked to assume roles and responsibilities that were unrelated to coaching and for which they felt unprepared. "As the year went on," says one coach at an elementary site, "I gradually came to be viewed more as a co-administrator than an instructional coach. I guess that made sense because I was essentially running the school for half the day and not doing much coaching."

Here is a simple task to help you to define boundaries. It will likely be a simple task, regardless of whether you are a novice coach or a seasoned veteran.

List on the left side of a piece of paper all of the tasks that you could be asked to do, or have been asked to do, that have little or no direct impact on improving a teacher's behavior. For example, distributing field trip notices to all classrooms has nothing to do with teacher improvement.

On the right side of the paper, write a short phrase that would describe the actual impact of doing each of the tasks you listed. Who or what would such a task impact? For example, for handing out notices, your actual impact would be that teachers have notices ready to give to students. Your completed list is essentially a ready-made rebuttal to the frustrations shared by hundreds of coaches in our surveys who abandoned coaching because it involved a lot more than coaching.

The Leaders Lounge

As a school or district leader, you are both responsible for initiating teacher change efforts as well as planning, organizing, staffing and monitoring them. Simultaneously, you are probably asked/told to support other change initiatives that you did not select, may not agree with, understand or care about. Look at the short list of leader characteristics below and circle the three you believe are most important if your primary responsibility to the school's instructional program is to change teacher behavior in a way that improves student learning.

Motivational	Persuasive
Articulate	Disciplined
Patient	Honest
Knowledgeable	Empathetic
Flexible	Visionary

We'll look more closely at the characteristics of a site leader who best maximizes positive teacher behavioral changes as we move through upcoming chapters.

Fun Quiz

1. An assumption is something I believe that guides my:

a. thinking
b. reactions
c. conduct
d. all of these

2. If we say something is logical, we mean that it
a. has a stable order
b. makes sense to me
c. is mathematical
d. is scientific

3. Referring to something as *parochial* means that it is
a. narrow or limited
b. old
c. bad
d. religious in nature

4. Scientific evidence shows that most people will change their behavior if presented with facts supporting the change.

       True   False   Not Sure

5. Traditional teacher development efforts endorse the assumption that

a. more is less   b. more is better   c. less is more   d. a and c

Chapter 2

Why Would Anyone Want To Change?

Introduction

It is hardly a revelation that most people do not enjoy change. Sure, there are some change efforts that are fun: vacationing more frequently, spending more time on an enjoyable hobby or with a special person. But when it comes to actually making a behavioral change – especially one that requires an increase of focus, effort or time – sometimes even a highly desirable outcome is not enough to motivate an individual to stick to it. Paradoxically, we are all about changes in other people; identifying areas of change for them, why they should change, how we think they should change, and when that change should occur (now, preferably). There are a variety of theories you may recall from your psychology classes about how and why people change. This chapter answers a critical question that is mostly neglected in educational change efforts:

What motivates individuals to change?

Objectives

In this chapter you will learn:

1. How structures of interpretation affect our motivation to change;

2. Who Alice, Biff and Carla are and why we need to understand each of them;

3. Why understanding these typologies is critical for designing individual and organizational change efforts;

4. That the failure of an organization to have a well-articulated theory of human change almost always results in no change, or at best, fragmented change that yields no system-wide improvement.

You've Probably Seen Or Heard This Before

It's 3:50 in the afternoon. It has been one of those Thursdays that seems to drag on forever. You are already more than an hour into a staff meeting that has been dominated by the principal's presentation of slide after countless PowerPoint slide of charts and graphs of test scores and statistics. Even the stick man figures on the slides – designed ostensibly for humor or amusement – have lost their diversionary power. After about the umpteenth slide showing some bar graph, scatter plot or line curve, the principal states the popular refrain that, "This graphic shows..." and moves to the next slide. You scan the room and notice the following: about a third of the staff has eyes that are glazed over from the charts and graphs. Another third is muttering under their breath that the charts do not show the true talents of students and are unfair. The final third of the staff appears to be genuinely interested in the principal's slideshow, especially the box that shows how standard deviations for reading scores in third grade appear larger than the prior school year, notwithstanding a slight change in the parabolic curve distribution of scores.

The meeting finally concludes – but not without another chant of "This graphic shows…" — and you make your way to the parking lot. As you walk along with four other teachers, you hear something like the following dialogue.

<u>Teacher A:</u> "Wow. My eyes are watering from those slides and all those numbers."

<u>Teacher B:</u> "I wish we could just teach the *whole* student and stop focusing so much on statistics and test results."

<u>Teacher C:</u> "Well, now I'm not at all sure what I'm supposed to be doing in math since our numbers are so low."

<u>Teacher D:</u> "What are you guys bringing tomorrow for the pot luck lunch?"

Why Should I Change?

Few people would disagree that continued improvement – whether as individuals, groups or organizations – is at least potentially a good thing. Who wouldn't want to be smarter, achieve a greater level of fitness, use time more productively, or have a larger vocabulary? But as we recall from our psychology classes and life's lessons, human change or improvement is much easier to talk about sometimes than to do. Indeed, it is alarming to see how many things people do that are known to be dangerous, bad for their health, or injurious to others, yet they keep on doing them. Maybe this isn't so surprising when studies have shown that nine of 10 people who survive a major heart surgery as a result of lifestyle choices (i.e., poor diet, smoking, drinking, no exercise, high stress) will by two years later not have changed their lifestyle.[1] A stunning percentage — almost 80% — of people who were prescribed a medication for lowering life-threatening cholesterol levels for the rest of their lives had ceased taking the medication after one year.[2] Almost 50 percent of the 37,000 study subjects quit taking the pill within two months. So why would these people not change their behaviors in the face of medical advice, and presumably the exhortations of loved ones? Why wouldn't these people make a change, even when it comes to saving their own lives?

As we delve into the shallows and depths of why and how people change, let's begin building a firm foundation for our work as coaches in this important area. Two important facts will guide us through the first section.

Fact 1: Organizations do not change. Only individuals can change. This precept gives rise to an analogous joke.

> *How do you move a cemetery?* Answer: *One body at a time.*

As a field research project, count at your next educational meeting the number of references to "school" "grade-level", "district", or "educational" change that you hear. Sorry, folks; none of those entities are changeable. The good news is that the people who comprise them –individual, free-thinking humans — can change.

Fact 2: Motivation to change comes before the change.
It is unlikely that most of us woke up today and decided to adopt a vegan diet, start training for a 26.2-mile marathon or commit to

reading all the classic literature of the world. Instead, we need a motivation to precede our change.

Psychology 101

It is usually through our experiences in college psychology courses that we learn in depth the myriad theories about human change. Names like Freud, Maslow, Jung and Skinner are usually foundational, though other names and ideas abound. Each of these big thinkers presents a paradigm, or way of thinking, about human change. Perhaps you already have a favorite, or maybe you have seen a certain theorist's ideas play out in your own life. Our discussion here seeks to help you to view these theories as falling into one of three categories with respect to their central thesis about how and why people change. With all due respect to these brilliant thinkers, we are now going to both summarize and elaborate on their respective theories in a way that helps us to better understand the why and how of changing teacher behavior for the better. Though brief, our review here will establish a very important base of understanding when we turn the corner shortly and talk about all of the teachers seated in your staff lounge and what makes them tick when it comes to personal and professional change.

Human Change Theories

Affective

Many human change and development theories are grounded in how people perceive and feel about themselves, others, their past and present, and the world around them. We all remember Maslow's pyramid (Hierarchy of Needs), where the apogee of human development is reaching a level referred to as "self-actualization." Though not visible, this is a subjective state of being experienced by the individual wherein they find peace with themselves, others and the world. This state of actualization is an affective state, experienced only by the individual. Other theories like humanism and self-empowerment all focus on how you are feeling about things. According to this view, affective evaluations of self, others and the world are the continuum along which humans progress. A change that is perceived as injurious to your feelings would be discarded in favor of a change that makes you feel good. Visit any thrift store or used book store to find shelves of self-help books that put affect at the center of their view of human development and change.

Behavioral

In his classic novel, *Walden Two*, behavioral psychologist B.F. Skinner described a utopian society controlled solely by operant conditioning that focused on getting certain desired behaviors from each member of the community. You may remember Pavlov's pooch, who gained fame and notoriety by salivating upon the presentation first of food, and then by the mere ringing of a bell. In short, Skinner generalized that all human behavior (and that of most other living creatures and organisms) could be controlled through methods of selective reinforcement. Under this umbrella, behaviors were not necessarily good or bad, but rather desirable or undesirable in a given context. No attention was paid to how one might feel or think about a change. Instead, we need merely find the proper reinforcement and get to work shaping the desired behavior.

Cognitive

Let's begin our refresher course with Freud and move on to Bandura, Jung and Dr. Phil. The paradigm here is that all human development and change rests on the ability and innate desire to cognitively make sense of ourselves, our relationships, our past and present, indeed, our place in the world. Psychoanalytic practices based on this view call for unraveling past events, thoughts and relationships to understand how they affect our thinking, actions and feelings today. Through this process of intellectual sense-making, we unleash our cerebral capacities to organize, catalog, describe, label and accept or dismiss things about ourselves or others. Different from affective theories that ask, "How did that make you feel," cognitive theories ask, "Why did you do that"? Central to this school of thought is that we, as humans, are intellectually capable of making sense of ourselves and orchestrating our own changes through our thinking processes.

We can see that each of these camps has a somewhat different take on human change and development. Much like watching a good lawyer movie, each argument sounds thoroughly sensible and convincing — until the next lawyer stands up and presents something new that makes perfect sense and is equally convincing. Certainly, theories are beautiful, and frequently elegant and alluring. But once we enter the real world, and our task becomes helping others to change, we recognize and think of new and sometimes confounding factors that were hidden from us in the Xanadu world of college textbooks. For example: Which of these theories works most quickly to change human behavior? What resources are needed for each theory, including time, money and patience? Which allow for clear goal-setting, so we will know if the goal has been reached? Are they all equally useful in an organization where the task is usually to change multiple players? What if people have actually learned to not change, or have been allowed to believe that change is optional and self-determined? These are difficult questions, most of which are ignored in educational settings.

But our challenge remains: we need to change teacher behavior in a way that benefits students, our school and our district as a whole. So, let's start by building what we will call a *unified theory of human change* that not only makes sense, but works to bring about relatively quick and sustainable teacher change. We'll do that by referring back to the first two facts of change that we presented at the outset of this chapter:

Fact 1: Only individuals can change.

Fact 2: All change is preceded by a motivation to change.

The emphasis for now is understanding how individuals get motivated to change. A fun way to synthesize the information that follows is to quickly jot down the names of five or six educators you know well, or that you have some experience with in meetings and such. You will now proceed to understand at a very deep level what makes them come alive or shut down when someone mentions the word "change".

Structures Of Interpretation

All of us hear, process and interpret information in different ways. Perhaps simplistic sounding at first, it turns out that scientists have learned that people can be grouped into categories based on how they interpret information, including messages that relate to changes. Known in psychology circles as structures of interpretation, our past experiences, our upbringing, and a host of other factors particular to each of us combine to serve as a screen or filter through which we take in information. These filters make us predisposed to hear certain things in a message, or to not hear certain things. Ultimately, our structure of interpretation greatly influences how we will react to the information or message.

But structures of interpretation are not the same for each person in a group, meaning that the same message can be interpreted by some people as an energizing bolt of lightning to change, while the same message is interpreted by others as ridiculous, misguided or injurious. Remember back to the staff meeting scenario at the beginning of this chapter? In that meeting, we saw that our well-intentioned principal assumed that everyone would react the same to the endless slideshow showing declining student achievement. The principal most likely assumed that this unfavorable data would light a fire under everyone to change. If only it were that simple for beings as complex as humans. The dialogue between staff members on the way to the parking lot shows us how different structures of interpretation radically affected each of their reactions to the presentation and their motivation to change.

Do you have the names of your fellow educators written down? Let's get to know them and their various structures of interpretation. Once we know this, light will shine brightly as we open the door to actually tapping into what motivates people to change.

Alice Affect

Alice Affect (or her counterpart, Alex Affect) wears her heart proudly on her sleeve. Information passes first through her ears and then seemingly directly to her heart, allowing her to quickly decide on its affective merits. In short, she feels or does not feel the message. What matters most to Alice is that the world is just, fair, equal and preferably a happy place. When she listens to arguments or presentations, she is attentive to their emotional quality and the effect they have on her emotions and those of others. If the exhortation is to change – whether as an individual or as part of a group – she first looks for and questions the story that surrounds the request. Does the change impact people positively or negatively? How will those affected by the change feel about it, both before, during and after its implementation? Is the change just and fair for all involved? To motivate Alice to change the message must resonate with her emotions and well up positive feelings that the change is affectively worthy of her efforts.

Biff Behavior

Biff Behavior (or his counterpart Brenda Behavior) is a person of action. Forget the meetings, forget the endless planning, the multi-hour PowerPoint presentations, the emotional discussions and the tears of joy or sorrow. Biff wants the bottom line: *What do you want me to do?* A lover of procedure, steps, organized processes and linear activity, Biff needs to know what works and what has worked. If it's not broken, don't fix it. But if it is broken, then decide on the action, tell him what to do, and let's get started. Like a carpenter, Biff wants the tools, the process and the outcome clearly defined. He hears messages in terms of the actions needed to bring something about and how to organize the resources to "git 'er done." If it's a change you want from Biff, tell him what it is, how you want it done, provide the materials needed and tell him when to start. Then check up on him soon because he wants to be sure he is doing it "right".

Carla Cognitive

For Carla Cognitive (or her counterpart, Carl Cognitive), it is all about facts, data, and provable statements that are unadorned and of unquestionable veracity. Carla appreciates and enjoys analysis so that she can quickly whittle incoming information down into its smallest and most persuasive elements of truth. Numbers, graphs, charts, mathematical analyses and research are what she listens for when people talk. If the message lacks these characteristics, she is apt to ignore the information or to criticize its lack of substance. She is prone to ask for the scientific basis of a statement or assertion, and she prefers to be provided with written material that she can study in detail to verify that it is indeed true. For Carla, the motivation to change her behavior begins with facts, a convincing argument or some analysis that shows action X is better than action Y. Motivation to change for her is a cognitive process, plain and simple, as clear and factual as 2 + 2= 4.

Back To The Staff Meeting

In our staff meeting vignette, you will recall that the principal was clicking off slide after slide showing student progress advances and declines, elaborating each with a numerical analysis. You are probably seeing in your mind a meeting like this wherein one third of the staff is dozing, one third is offended by the distillation of human beings into numbers, and the final third is wondering if the charts mean they are supposed to do something differently. Most important, you can see why structures of interpretation either open the door of possibility to change or slam it shut. Like in many meetings, the leader of the group favored his own structure of interpretation — usually unwittingly — much to the detriment of the other two types sitting in the group who heard nothing to motivate them to change.

Listen to this snippet of another meeting where the leader is a savvy student of how structures of interpretation are the front line in the challenge of human change.

You can see from this slide that our math scores have improved in several grades where we implemented the Math Exploration Program. Parents of students in those rooms have come to my office practically in tears to describe how much their children's fear of math has changed to one of excitement and wonder. My observations of these classrooms have shown that the simple, five-step process for teaching inquiry in this program relies on a clear, easy-to-use student workbook that methodically allows the teacher to maximize small-group attention. The fact that math scores in these grades increased by 24% relative to other grades not using the program, with a much smaller standard deviation, shows that we have evidence here of something that can work for all of us.

Even from this segment, you can see how all of our staff lounge friends — Alice Affect, Biff Behavior and Carla Cognitive — heard in the message what they needed to activate their motivation to do something differently. Alice heard about the emotional impact on students, Biff knows there's a solid procedure and materials, and Carla got her standard deviation. For the principal, the teachers and the students, it's a win-win-win. We have tapped into the first step of human change: finding a motivation. Below are some examples of how different typologies interpret messages differently.

Affective Typology – Alice

What Was Said	Initial Interpretation	Motivation to Change
The district said students from our campus are consistently unprepared for their high school classes.	It isn't right to send students to high school unprepared. We need to do something different so that our students are set up for success.	This strong emotional message resonates well with Alice. She feels for the students' situation and wants to fix it.
The district says we need to implement a new writing program because our current system isn't working.	That isn't fair. The students love our writing units. They should come see their creativity.	As the statement lacks an emotional message, Alice doesn't hear a reason to change and instantly defends her current practice through her affective lens.
The district said that more than half of our eighth graders received a D or lower in their freshman English classes.	The transition to high school can be hard for students. What are the ninth-grade teachers doing to support them? Maybe they're being too tough on the kids.	As the statement lacks an emotional message, Alice doesn't hear a reason to change and instantly justifies the presented data through her affective lens.

Behavioral Typology – Biff

What was Said	Initial Reaction	Motivation to Change
The district said students from our campus are consistently unprepared for their high school classes.	That isn't good. What am I supposed to do differently?	As the statement lacks a clear directive, Biff doesn't hear a reason to change so will continue doing business as usual.
The district says we need to implement a new writing program because our current system isn't working.	If you say it's broken, then let's get to work fixing it.	A clear directive resonates well with Biff. He wants to implement the new program the right way and right now.
The district said that more than half of our eighth graders received a D or lower in their freshman English classes.	We are using the district-adopted curriculum. The ninth-grade teachers must not be using the curriculum correctly.	Biff readily accepts the conclusion but does not hear a clear action plan for him to follow.

Cognitive Typology – Carla

What was Said	Initial Reaction	Motivation to Change
The district said students from our campus are consistently unprepared for their high school classes.	That is one perspective. What data are you using to support it?	As the statement lacks any data or analysis, Carla doesn't hear a reason to change and instantly looks for data to justify making a change to her current practices.
The district says we need to implement a new writing program because our current system isn't working.	What data do they have that shows that the old program is not working? What evidence shows a new program will be better?	The statement lacks any solid data for Carla to consider a change. She will continue with her current practices.
The district said that more than half of our eighth graders received a D or lower in their freshman English classes.	This isn't good. If most of our students are not able to pass their English classes, we need to make a change.	The strong data-driven conclusion resonates well with Carla. She accepts that something different is needed.

Things To Ponder Or Discuss

1. How persuasive are numbers and other data for you when it comes to changing your teaching practices? Why is this such a predominant approach in public education?

2. Have you ever wondered why school or district change initiatives seem to so brazenly disregard basic psychological elements of human change?

3. Do you believe that people have a limited amount of motivation to change, and thus it should be treated with great care?

4. What did you learn from your analysis of the group of teachers you listed and their probable structures of interpretation?

5. Are there some people who are combinations of Alice, Biff and Carla? How can you tell?

The Coaches Corner

As a coach, you will on a daily basis be trying to identify teachers' motivations to change their behavior. But a good place to start before working with teachers is to have a good understanding of your own structure of interpretation. Are you more like Alice, Biff or Carla? Are you particularly prototypical of one of these typologies, or might you be someone who has more of one and some of another? Take a while and really think about how you respond to change messages. The learning for you here is to be aware that when you talk to teachers — about most anything related to instruction, learning and change — you are likely to fall back on your own structure of interpretation. But to awaken the motivators in the teachers with whom you work, you need to be *trilingual* and speak the languages of Alice, Biff and Carla. You may even recognize in yourself certain tendencies to be more like Carla at work and Biff at home. Utilize this insight as you get to know your teachers.

Many coaches report that working with a teacher of the same structure of interpretation can be easier, while working with a structure outside of your own requires forethought and prior planning. With practice, you can be comfortable and effective with Alice, Biff and Carla.

The Leaders Lounge

Read again both staff meeting vignettes. Do you see yourself in any of these with respect to which of the structures of interpretation you tend to project? Would your staff members say your meetings and messages resonate more with the Alices, the Biffs or the Carlas? What have been the results of your efforts to motivate others to change as seen through the lens of this study of structures of interpretation?

Is it possible that your dominant structure of interpretation bears some link to the lack of motivation of some members of your staff to consider a change?

Fun Quiz

1. The study of human psychology is considered what kind of science?
a. social
b. behavioral
c. physical
d. applied

2. The best synonym for the verb *to motivate* is:
a. to force
b. to encourage
c. to incite
d. to develop

3. If we present lots of facts to teachers and then expect them to change, we are assuming that change is solely a _____ process.
a. behavioral
b. cognitive
c. intellectual
d. linear

4. Groups cannot change; only _____ can change.
a. people
b. organizations
c. individuals
d. systems

5. Within the concept of *structures of interpretation*, we can refer to Alice, Biff and Carla as _____.
a. staff members
b. stereotypes
c. metaphors
d. typologies

Chapter 3
It's All About Behavior

Introduction

As the old saying goes, the road to hell is paved with good intentions. In this chapter we address head on what is likely to be one of the most provocative elements of our Performance-Based Coaching™ model: specifically, that people must behave their way into change. It is not enough for them to think about change, or to feel good about a change. We have seen countless coaching programs that are guided by a range of philosophies and hoped-for outcomes, least of which is an observable change for the better in teacher behavior. When anything other than improved teacher performance is the primordial goal of coaching, the barn door is open to numerous distractions. Much money and time is squandered as individuals, committees, planning groups and task forces talk about change, plan for change, hope for change, attend change conferences or hypothesize about change. While all of these activities can make for interesting and stimulating conversations, they mask the singular and only factor that makes a difference for students, namely, improved teacher performance. And that is all about changing behavior.

Objectives

In this chapter you will learn:

1. Why most professional development efforts don't bring about organizational changes;

2. Why the failure of an organization to have a well-articulated theory of human change results in no change, or at best, fragmented change that yields no system-wide improvement;

3. Why behavior is the only thing that matters in the beginning, in the middle and in the end;

4. How to break reinforcing loops that keep people doing what they have always done;

5. Why teachers will first not like your approach, then come to not being able to live without it (and you).

You've Probably Seen Or Heard This Before

A large urban high school in Phoenix, Arizona, implemented a school-wide professional development program aimed at increasing students' ability to answer questions verbally in more academic ways. To do this, teachers participated in a multi-year training program to teach them how to improve the quality, clarity and specificity of their classroom questioning. Few disagreed with the conclusion that students were generally passive in class when it came to responding to teachers' questions. More than 80 hours of out-of-class professional development over a three-year period was provided to teachers in the theory, research and application of questioning skills to better involve students.

At the mid-point of the third year of implementation, the principal and several district administrators visited a variety of classrooms at the school to see how well the new information, methods and teacher behaviors had been implemented. Their visits devastated them. Almost 75% of the teachers (68 of the 90 teachers) made little to no use of what they had been exposed to in training. Of the 25% (22 actual teachers) who were implementing the information, half of them did it in a way that looked very different from how it was demonstrated in training sessions. The site's two instructional coaches could have anticipated the findings. Asked to interpret the poor results found during the visit, the two coaches highlighted three specific areas.

"For starters," said Brenda, a former language arts teacher turned site coach for all three years of the implementation, "no one ever told the teachers they had to do it. So, many of the teachers never tried anything, even when we scheduled coaching sessions to help them." Rob, the other site coach who had previously been a very successful math teacher at the school, continued. "Most of the teachers told us they were still thinking about trying it or that they felt the strategies did not feel right for their teaching style."

"The second thing we kept seeing," said Brenda, "was that those teachers who tried it right away and wanted to get it right struggled initially, and many stopped trying after it didn't work the way they were told it would. Some teachers in this group just did what they could, which usually resulted in lots of modifications."

"What was the third reason?" asked the district staff development director and the person who led the three-year effort. Brenda and

Rob looked at one another and then looked away from the small group. "Well, we need to know," said the director. "It's hard to discuss," said Brenda," though Rob and I have discussed it a hundred times. The truth is neither the teachers, nor the administrators here – not even Rob and I ourselves — ever had a clear idea of how we were going to get all these teachers to change. They knew there would be coaching, but no one knew what that should look like or what it should accomplish." "We are both good teachers," said Rob, "but I'm not sure I would have understood how coaching was supposed to help if I were one of the teachers involved. Unfortunately, we never knew what to tell them to clear that up."

A Unified Theory Of Human Change

You will recall from the previous chapter that we explored why anyone would be motivated to consider and then attempt a change in the first place. Even the most motivated of individuals can be thwarted in their effort to change if the people and the organization in which they work provides unclear, confusing, or no communication about exactly what they are expected to change and how that change will happen. It is worrisome that so many educational institutions regularly expect the people in them to change – quickly, by themselves, and on demand – but are bereft of any clear theory of how people change. Let that sink in for a moment. We are going to invest large sums of money and hundreds of hours into a plan that we want to result in some human behavioral change. But oops! We forgot to actually have a theory or clearly articulated philosophy that will guide our efforts to change that most beguiling of creatures — the human being.

The word "theory" is simultaneously revered and deplored by educators and the general populace. Theories, for some, smack of pie-in-the-sky musings that have little relation to reality. For others, theory is everything, since theories are explanations of how things work. Whatever your view, all of our lives are governed by a set of general theories, and a complex web of personal theories. Let's define this word clearly and then explore why theories are so important to us, even if we sometimes outwardly eschew them.

The term "theory" is properly defined as the formulation of general principles that explain the operation or functioning of some phenomena, supported by considerable evidence. Theories are sometimes confused with "hypotheses", which are tentative explanations of a phenomenon with an inadequacy of evidence for its support. Rounding out the triumvirate of related terms is "idea", which is nothing more than a mental conception, notion, opinion or belief. The differences between these terms is crucial to understand. Theories, for their part, usually reflect a great deal of thinking and some attempt to link all or parts of them to the real world. Theories also usually come with a list of related terms and definitions, along with some explanation of the various components of the theory and the relationships between them.

Let's look at a simple theory that impacts all of us at the start of each day. From commercials to documentaries to physicians' warnings, we are told that breakfast is the most important meal of the day. Proponents of this theory have their arguments, while those in disagreement have theirs. Is there definitive proof that eating breakfast is better (more desirable, more healthy, more X) than not eating breakfast? The answer is no. But all of us made a decision today to eat or not eat breakfast based on some theory we have heard or formulated. Chances are, as an adult you have come to be either a "breakfast eater" or "not a breakfast eater". It is a theory that guides your behavior. This link between theory and behavior is an important one for understanding at a deep level how people change.

Extending the example just a bit further, you probably have foisted your breakfast theory onto your children, spouse, friends or others.

Whether you backed it up with research, anecdote or edict we will never know. Have you ever tried to convert a *non-breakfaster* to a *breakfaster,* or vice versa? As with most of our personal theories, mine are best, correct and should be adopted by you. By way of beating this analogy just a bit more, we all have theories that cover everything in our lives: a theory of driving, of marriage, of child-rearing, of television viewing, of yard care and on and on. Taken together, our own theories are usually integrated and consistent, or what we could call *unified.* By contrast, imagine having no theories to guide your life, or changing theories every couple of weeks? Think for a moment about how many times you have explained your theories to your children, friends, or to anyone who would listen? Have you ever been frustrated by having to utilize a theory that contradicts your own? All of these questions take us back to teacher development at your school or district and end with a million-dollar question:

What is the unified theory of human change that guides our change efforts?

For most educational organizations, the answers cover the gamut from no theory to mixed theories to confusing theories to the theory of the day. Remember our breakfast example from the previous paragraph? If we have a theory about that, shouldn't we put in the time and effort to develop a theory for the change effort we are going to unleash on our teachers? What we are talking about here is defining the principles that explain how human beings stop doing something and begin doing something new or different. This is not a 100-page document, nor is it a 20-unit package of courses at the university. Rather, it is first and foremost a discussion at the leadership level of an organization about what we believe about human change. Why do people change? How do people change? What do they need to change? When should they change? Who can change? What are the relationships between people that facilitate or discourage change? What are the roles and responsibilities of the various people in the organization?

As we saw in our vignette, the coaches hit the bullseye when they gave their reasons for the poor implementation of the high school's three-year training program aimed at getting teachers to ask questions differently. What they described was an organization with no clear or unified theory of human change, which is frequently characterized by the following attributes:

- Leaders make no formal call for teachers to change

- Mixed, confusing or contradictory messages come from leaders about the change

- No clear view of how organizational personnel and resources will be organized to help teachers with the change

- Teachers are not provided with information about the organization's unified theory of human change

- Poor or no implementation of the change across the organization

- Rapid loss of interest by most members to implement the change

- Coaches, teachers and administrators who are unsure of what role coaches play, what coaching is to accomplish, and how coaches are to fill their days

Working as an instructional coach in this type of environment can be extremely frustrating, since their efforts are seen as just another part of something that lacks logic, definition and explanation. But we can change this condition by establishing and explaining to our teachers a unified theory of human and organizational change that builds heavily on:

- what is known about people

- empirical evidence about how those people stop and start new behaviors

- common sense

- *Dancing With the Stars.*

Let's begin with three principles that will form part of our unified theory of human change.

Principle 1: Reinforcing loops can encourage or discourage adopting new behaviors.

Principle 2: You must behave your way into change; you can't feel or think your way there.

Principle 3: Most of us can't change ourselves by ourselves.

Remember back to the three typologies of people in your staff lounge? We affectionately referred to them as *Alice Affect, Biff Behavior* and *Carla Cognitive.* Let's visit them again, but this time we will listen to them and watch them working in two different contexts; the first is at a school with no unified theory of human change. The second school has a unified theory of human change that is comprised of our first three principles. Recall that our teachers have been asked to attend a three-year staff development progression to help them to develop better student questioning skills. After the first two full days of training, listen to each of them reflect on what they have learned.

Version 1:

This school has no unified theory of human change.

Alice Affect

"I can see some benefits for my students in this approach, but I am worried that calling on students by name and without them volunteering could really be embarrassing for them. I know I wouldn't want someone to do that to me."

Biff Behavior

"It seems like a pretty straightforward approach to things. I think I can get this started tomorrow and be up and running with everything by the end of the week."

Carla Cognitive

"The presenters did a good job, but I did not hear much research base for this approach. I also noticed that they did not provide the names of other schools that are trying this and the scores they achieved after doing it."

Three weeks later, we stop in to visit each of their classrooms. Alice is not calling on students by name and still waits for volunteers. Biff has radically modified what he learned in a way that is bulky and not similar to the training demonstrations. Carla has not implemented any of the new questioning techniques. When asked to explain their current level of implementation, the answers are predictable. "I think this method is intimidating for students and could really hurt their self-esteem," says Alice. "I did what I learned at the training," says

Biff. "I'm still waiting on more student data information before I start," says Carla. Multiply this across the whole campus, and we have a failed implementation that is characteristically reflective of having no unified theory of human change. It also illustrates another important concept: how reinforcing loops can cause us to replicate behaviors that we have always done – and to feel good about them.

Reinforcing loops are a powerful way of understanding human behavior. Essentially, a reinforcing loop happens when something that I believe is going to happen actually happens – at least through my eyes. When this information is consistent with the way I already believe — let's call this a mental model — then my initial belief is confirmed, and my mental model remains intact and ready for the next onslaught of information. As humans, we tend to take facts and fit them into the mental models we already have. If those facts don't fit nicely into our existing models, we tend to be dismissive of them, disparage them, or deny them entirely. Here's an example of how reinforcing loops serve to maintain our mental models. Alice believes the new questioning methods are a self-esteem killer for students. Believing this, her efforts at trying the new behavior reinforce what she already thinks. She is hesitant to call on students randomly, and it only takes one or two students to appear to be uncomfortable for her to double down on her *a priori* conclusion.

Biff, our teacher of action, immediately gets to work on the methods, but finds that he did not remember everything from the training and that students are not immediately responsive to the new approach. He soldiers on, but quickly concludes that the methods are not clear enough for him and his students. His extreme modifications look more like the way he has always questioned students. The reinforcing loop at work here is that the training (and the trainer, and the district, and the publishers of the materials, and...) did not provide enough structure for him to immediately implement with success. His limited and solo classroom experiment showed him that he is correct.

Carla is still waiting for the research and so delays implementation. Her belief is that ideas without numbers and studies are just hypotheses, ideas or opinions. When that information is never provided, or not in a form she trusts, her reinforcing loop is confirmed: this is just another teaching fad that lacks serious and rigorous science. She happily avoids the new practices, confident that she has saved her students and herself from another ill-informed instructional whim.

The diagram below shows how reinforcing loops serve to do just what they say they do: they reinforce what we always thought, they substantiate our existing theories, and they allow us to continue doing what we have always done. With each new iteration of the loop, we become more confident in our existing mental models and their related behaviors and more committed to their enduring utility.

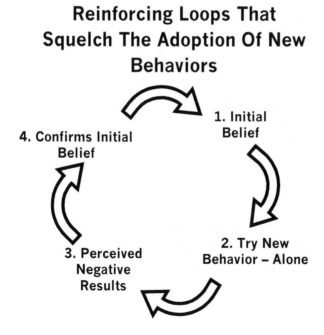

Reinforcing Loops That Squelch The Adoption Of New Behaviors

1. Initial Belief

2. Try New Behavior – Alone

3. Perceived Negative Results

4. Confirms Initial Belief

Version 2:

This school has a unified theory of human change that is well communicated.

Let's visit our friends again but imagine they are at a different school. They are still implementing the same student questioning program. But at this school, they are working within the principles we stated earlier that comprise a part of our unified theory of human change. Specifically, this school's theory holds that:

Principle 1: Reinforcing loops can encourage or discourage adopting new behaviors.

Principle 2: You have to behave your way into change; you can't feel or think your way there.

Principle 3: Most of us can't change ourselves by ourselves.

Because of these principles, the two school site coaches have been working with teachers in a very different way. Each of their visits has required teachers to implement some part of the questioning methods, regardless of their current opinions or feelings about the program. The teachers have heard a detailed and well-articulated presentation of how district leaders view human change. They were able to ask questions and discuss with other teachers the implications of the unified theory. Supported by their principal's clear declaration that all teachers will implement these methods, the coaches enter each classroom with a clear objective: to improve the teacher's behavior relative to the questioning program they are learning. Everyone is clear that student improvement will come about because of specific changes in teacher behavior.

We visit their classrooms three weeks after the training and observe the following.

Alice Affect

Alice is calling on students randomly, though her facial winces show she is uncomfortable with this new behavior. Still, she perseveres through the lesson and we see no students crying.

Biff Behavior

Biff is reaching a high level of proficiency with the first two steps of the questioning technique. His coaches have narrowed his focus to the first two steps of the questioning process and their collaborative efforts are paying off. Biff asks better questions and receives more articulate answers from students.

Carla Cognitive

Carla is using the methods exactly as written in the directions. We notice that when each student answers, she is noting something on a page next to her lesson plans. Her coaches have helped her to design a system for collecting data from her own class related to the results of the new questioning methods. She has proudly reported to some members of her department that her findings are encouraging.

Here's what we didn't see on our visits, but it has consumed almost all of the coaches' time with these teachers. Knowing that each of these teachers initially had expressed reservations about using the new methods, the coaches intervened in the reinforcing loop. If allowed to try the new methods alone, the coaches knew that each teacher's initial belief would likely be reinforced by perceived negative results, thus completing the loop in a negative way. But since behavioral change was their sole focus, the coaches knew that only by having people try a new behavior with assistance can they restructure these existing reinforcing loops.

The coaches relied on psychological evidence that people can actually "try out" new behaviors that are uncomfortable for them by doing them in collaboration with someone more expert, thus "objectifying" the behavior instead of personalizing it. In simple terms, the coaches' interventions were aimed at helping teachers to "perceive" the outcomes differently, as positive instead of negative. As Alice sees students answer more frequently and hears from typically silent students whose faces beam when they have the correct answer, she is seeing that a change in her behavior (calling on students randomly) is bringing about a positive change in her students and in the effectiveness of her teaching. Her behaviors, albeit uncomfortable for her, are causing her to feel differently about this method and that it actually can be a self-esteem builder for students. Her reinforcing loop is now being reconstructed with the skillful guidance of a couple of savvy coaches working within a well-articulated unified theory of human and organizational change.

For his part, Biff was coached to focus on small steps first, gradually building up to the entirety of the process. Through this approach, Biff's actual behavior has been far more skilled, leading to a higher level of enthusiasm for the methods is high for both he and his students.

Carla wanted research, so her smart-thinking coaches put her in the center of her own research project. By seeing her own students answer questions in ways she had not seen before in response to her utilization of new behaviors, she is learning that she can get the data she wants from right in her own classroom.

The reinforcing loop below is almost the same as the one on an earlier page, but notice how the coaches' interventions, working within the school's unified theory of human change, have changed the reinforcing aspect of the loop.

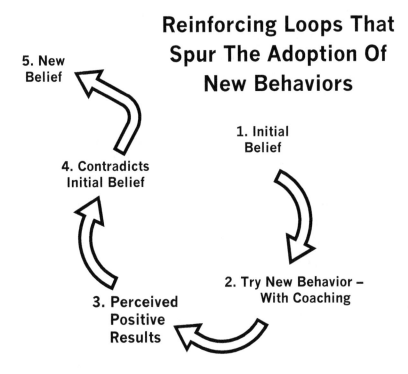

Reinforcing Loops That Spur The Adoption Of New Behaviors

5. New Belief

4. Contradicts Initial Belief

1. Initial Belief

3. Perceived Positive Results

2. Try New Behavior – With Coaching

How Behavior Changes Hearts And Minds — and Improves Dancing

Have you ever noticed that on the popular television show *Dancing with the Stars* there is little effort aimed at providing a research base for *The Cha-Cha* or emotional pleas for *The Tango*? It's a neat idea to think that teachers – or people, or novice dancers – will change their behavior based upon the right piece of information, learning about a great process or hearing a heart-melting emotional plea. But if the goal for our organization – comprised of the humans within it – is to bring about improved conditions for learning and student achievement, then we need to get on with the behavioral changes necessary to realize those important outcomes. We simply do not have enough time, resources or patience to have everyone eventually think or feel their way into a change. *Dancing with the Stars* would be a years-long series if they had to find just the right research or the right emotional plea to motivate each dancer to strap on their boogie shoes and hit the dance floor.

In few words, changing hearts and minds is best and most efficiently accomplished by helping people to try the new behavior with lots of support. When they see – sometimes quickly and sometimes over the long term – that their behavioral change brought about something better in their students, then we as coaches have successfully intervened in an existing reinforcement loop that likely would have never caused them to behave differently or to adopt a new method or behavior.

We will explore in later chapters how performance-oriented coaches organize and support teachers to try new behaviors and how to use those vital experiences to help them to see new things in their students and in themselves. When coaches work within an organization that has a well-articulated and unified theory of human change, it's another win-win-win for teachers, students and the organization as a whole.

Things To Ponder Or Discuss

1. Describe the closest thing you have seen in your career to an organization having a unified theory of human change.

2. Which of the two versions of the high school change project are most familiar to you based on your experiences in public education?

3. Why do more school and district leaders not tell teachers that a change is required, or at least, expected?

4. Do humans prefer knowing what to expect from something (say, coaching) or are surprises preferable for most?

5. What openings for dissension, rejection or confusion arise when school and district leaders do not inform people of how their change will be managed?

6. Have you ever thought previously about common behaviors being the product of multiple iterations of reinforcing loops?

7. How might your answer to the previous question explain schools or districts where most teachers view change as entirely optional or not needed?

8. Is it possible, preferable, or impossible for a school or district to have an *eclectic unified theory of human change*?

9. What is the attraction educational organizations have to eclectic theories of everything?

The Coaches Corner

It only takes a few days on the job as a coach to understand if you are working within an organization that has a unified theory of human change that is regularly communicated, or if you are lost in a wilderness of confusion, contradictions, mixed messages or eclecticism. As coaches, you are both fish and fowl, student and docent, fellow teacher and change agent. These are big jobs that can be made either easier or more difficult by the existence or absence of a unified theory of human change like we discussed in this chapter. Here is an interesting task that will help you and your organizational leaders to better understand your historic role, and the role that you could play, as a Performance-Based Coach™.

Divide a piece of paper down the middle with a line. On the left side, list as many of the specific behaviors you have done as a coach as you can recall. For example, if you regularly walk students to the cafeteria, that is a behavior to list. If you are in charge of a small student group twice a day, write that down. If you meet with and coach three teachers per day, write that down. We are trying to craft a list of behaviors that fully represents your role as coach. If you're new to the coaching role, write the tasks or behaviors people have told you correspond to your job. Once completed with the left side, use the right column to identify for each item you listed what it reflects or implies about changing the behavior of humans. Look at the entirety of the right-side analyses when you are done and see if you can summarize those into what is currently the theory of human change in which you work.

The Leaders Lounge

The existence or non-existence of a unified theory of human change affects almost every element of your organization and of your leadership. If there is no theory that is widely known, you are in the cockpit of a jetliner with 40 other pilots seated in the rows behind you. They are flying their own jets. By contrast, if you have articulated a theory of human change to the members of your organization, how well have they understood it? List three key elements of your theory of change (or the theory/non-theory you inherited from the last administration if you are new to the site or district). For each of these elements, what implications do you see that directly impact the daily routines and functions of instructional coaches at your site? What inconsistencies can you identify in your theory that, if corrected, would benefit your coaches, teachers and students?

And by the way, if your unified theory of human change is not written down, you probably don't have one. Or at least you don't have one that anyone will recall accurately. Have you ever played *The Telephone Game?*

Fun Quiz

1. A reinforcing loop can also be referred to as a
    a. schemata
    b. mental model
    c. hypothesis
    d. system

2. All of these words are synonyms for the word *unified* except
    a. integrated
    b. logically related
    c. organized
    d. scientific

3. Freud believed that _____ preceded behavioral change.
    a. self-analysis
    b. therapy
    c. introspection
    d. ego

4. A theory is different than a hypothesis.

    True   False

5. In my opinion, most human change is
    a. linear
    b. circular
    c. recursive
    d. systematic
    e. something else

Chapter 4
When Change Is Needed, Help Is Required

Introduction

By now, we have traversed many of the most slippery slopes related to human change. Slippery because we as humans are good at saying one thing, thinking something altogether different, and actually doing it quite another way. The coaching of teachers can be one of those slippery slopes, even though the idea of working collaboratively with others sounds good initially. But after the honeymoon with the amorphous idea of coaching is over, a host of concerns, complaints, fire alarms and smokescreens can appear. Indeed, it is amazing to witness how many good reasons can be surfaced to *not* do coaching, or to *not* involve me in coaching. Given a choice, many of us would prefer to implement a change alone; that way, no one is watching. But, of course, all the research and the great majority of real life is against us here. The bottom line is that we are social beings. Having other people with us can make for a better birthday party, a more enjoyable theatre experience and even enhance our ability to learn new things. In this chapter we look specifically at the role others play in helping us to change, and we explore some provocative ideas about things like stress, self-esteem, collaboration and why we will only deal with experts on those things that matter most to us or that could cost us a lot of money if we get it wrong.

Objectives

In this chapter you will learn:

1. How others help us to change;

2. The eight questions that should be asked of any coaching approach before it is implemented;

3. How coaching can both sound and look different based on its underlying theoretical orientation;

4. How experts help us to change properly, more quickly, and in more lasting ways;

5. Why really great coaches are worth far more to their organizations than the actual money they earn;

6. Why Performance-Based Coaching™ brings about faster, more measurable and more sustainable human change than other coaching approaches.

You've Probably Heard Or Seen This Before

All of us want to do something better. Whether it be cooking, volleyball or being more outgoing, elevating our performance is a never-ending goal. But for most anything we want to improve upon, we usually must turn for help to someone more skilled than we currently are. Consider the following scenario from one of our families, which may remind you of something similar.

Karen and Daren both had an interest in tennis and practiced regularly. When they played each other, they usually split the matches. When both entered high school and were members of their respective school teams, each desperately wanted to be the best on the team. But the approaches they took to reach that goal were very different.

Karen played against a regular line-up of other girls on her team and some playing partners from local courts. Almost always, she was victorious and found the consistent winning a boon to her confidence. She received much verbal praise from parents and other players and found the adoration to be both motivating and rewarding.

Daren took another route. He asked the coach if he could practice against players from the varsity squad who were clearly better than he was. He also spent weekends at local courts playing against the best people who would accept his invitations. By his own admission, he lost far more matches than he won against this competition. He wasn't always happy about it, but he knew he was challenging himself. And even though he didn't win as much, his tennis skills were sharpened quickly by the strong competition and pointers he received from the superior players.

When it came time to play against players of the same level during each of their school tennis seasons, Daren quickly established himself as one of the better singles players in the league. Karen won occasionally but slid to the middle of the pack. Certainly, there are many factors that could partially explain this, but what seemed quite clear to coaches and the kids' parents was that Daren got better by playing against people who were better than him. From them, he learned techniques and strategies that he applied to his own developing game. Karen's skills stayed about the same, since her adversaries were either her equals or of lesser skill. She also sometimes overestimated her abilities because she was so used to winning.

There are two important principles to this story that bear directly on coaching teachers.

Principle 1: We get better by working on a task with others who are more knowledgeable or skillful than we currently are.

Principle 2: We don't have to be best friends with the people who help us the most to improve.

As we move into the application portion of this book, both of the principles above are important to understand, since Performance-Based Coaching™ differs dramatically in this regard – as well as in other ways — from other coaching theories and approaches you may be familiar with.

Comparing Approaches

Up to this point, we have laid a solid foundation for the theory and principles related to changing human behavior. We have emphasized that to change an organization like a school requires that the people in it change. Thus, how we approach individual change has much to do with how successful our organizational change efforts will be. Again, this is another important principle that is foundational for any coaching approach. After all, if the coaching approach and methods can't or don't consistently help individuals to improve, then the organization in which those people work is not likely to improve either. It is fashionable in education circles to give lip service to "system-wide" change. In reality, a system-wide change is the sum of all the individual changes in the organization. So now we're back to seeing the importance of successfully managing these two parallel and mutually reinforcing processes: individual change and organizational change.

Like most areas of knowledge dealing with human beings, there are other theories and approaches to bringing about change. We described several of the more popular ones in an earlier chapter. This is a good time to briefly look at some of these other coaching approaches and their underlying philosophies related to human change. But before embarking on that analysis, it is helpful to have a framework for evaluating the potential and actual outcomes that are associated with each approach. To do that, the list below provides eight important criteria for evaluating the utility of any coaching model that purports to improve either teacher performance, organizational performance, or both. We refer to both of these goals generally as bringing about some intended "change." The graphic below shows this relationship.

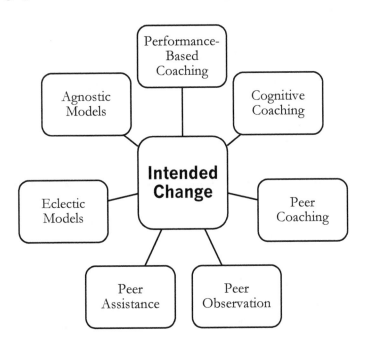

The eight criteria below provide educators, board members, researchers, funding agencies and other interested parties with a framework through which to evaluate these approaches and their intended and unintended consequences *before* implementation.

Eight Criteria For Evaluating The Effectiveness Of A Coaching Approach

1. The coaching approach makes the change (defined as a new behavior) happen quickly.

2. The change (the new behavior) is objectively measurable by others through visual or auditory information (see it or hear it). Nothing is subjective.

3. The change is sustainable.

4. The change contributes to meeting an organizational goal.

5. The change is implemented system-wide.

6. The coach is highly skilled in the knowledge and behaviors they coach.

7. The cost of bringing about the change is organizationally feasible.

8. The value of the coach responsible for bringing about change is greater than their cost to the organization.

Unfortunately, there does not seem to be a funny or memorable acronym to be made to help us remember these eight elements, but their basis in common sense will help. We frequently find that schools and districts fail to use such a checklist for evaluating the efficacy and practicality of a coaching initiative. Instead, it is more the case that an approach is selected for less-than-sound reasons: it's fun, it's easy, it's cheap, it was mentioned at a conference or meeting, it fits our current personnel, someone told us to use it. Unfortunately, such short-sighted analysis and simplistic reasoning usually results in poor results, wasted resources, and teachers and coaches who get little from the undertaking. In the worst case, a poorly-chosen approach can poison the water for sometimes years for any further attempts at coaching.

Let's now look briefly at some other coaching approaches and their underlying philosophies. We will then compare and contrast them to determine which approach best meets the eight characteristics of effective coaching that maximizes individual and organizational change.

Cognitive Coaching

Though used generically to refer to similar approaches, Cognitive Coaching[SM],[1] is described by its developers as "a process, a set of strategies, and a way of thinking that supports the ongoing development of individuals and organizations." Through this process, coaches and coachees strive to become increasingly self-directed and reflective. From their own website, the authors posit that:

"We all have resources that enable us to grow and change from within. The person being coached, not the coach, evaluates what is good or poor, appropriate or inappropriate, effective or ineffective about his/her work."[2]

As can be deduced from the characteristics above, this approach places great emphasis on individuals' ability to reason their way to improvement, largely through reflection and discussion with a coach who listens more than directs or intervenes.

Peer Coaching

This approach shares much in common with cognitive coaching but places more emphasis on the affective nature of the relationship between the coach and the teacher. Peer coaching, as described by its proponents, is a confidential process through which two or more professional colleagues work together to reflect on current practices. Through this relationship they expand, refine, and build new skills by sharing ideas and by teaching each other. They sometimes conduct classroom research or seek solutions to common problems or challenges. Although peer coaching seems to be the most prominent label for this type of activity, a variety of other names are used in schools to describe the same approach: peer support, consulting colleagues, peer sharing, and peer caring.

Great efforts are made in this approach to ensure there are no power connotations. Some claim the word "coaching" implies that one person in the collaborative relationship has a different status. This term may imply to some an inequality among colleagues that is inconsistent with the historical norm of public education, which can be considered to be nonhierarchical in structure within the teaching ranks. This approach also allows and encourages customization. From one website, we learn that, "Peer coaching is as individual and unique as the people who engage in it."[3]

Other salient aspects of this approach are that:

- The coach may have less expertise than the person being coached.

- Both the teacher and the coach decide the direction of the coaching.

- The relationship between coach and teacher is of supreme importance.

- Coaching must be pragmatic.

- Coaching is a learning experience both for coach and teacher.

- Coaching must be adapted to fit individuals – it's not a technique, it's a principle-shaped ontological stance and not a series of techniques.[4]

Peer Observation And Assistance

This approach "is designed to help teachers improve student achievement by increasing the teachers' awareness of the classroom techniques they are using and by teaching them to set goals for constructive changes and to assess the results of the changes that they make."[5] This approach emphasizes that participation is voluntary. In practice, it involves analyzing one's own teaching techniques together with a fellow teacher. Like the approaches previously described, proponents stress that this approach "does not threaten her (the teacher's) self-esteem" and "places the teacher in control of improving her existing skills or of developing new skills."[6]

Other characteristics of this approach are:

- One teacher gives feedback to the other by affirming the positive aspects of the other's teaching behavior.

- Reducing anxiety about the process is important, since a teacher with no or low anxiety is more likely to make desirable changes, thus enhancing motivation to adopt some new approaches or techniques.

- The approach in general seeks to reduce what Festinger calls "cognitive dissonance", referring to the stress and conflict one can experience when trying to do something new or different.[7]

- The teacher selects the skill to be worked on. Teacher decides if data is accurate or not.

Eclectic Models Of Coaching

Eclecticism refers to the picking, choosing and melding together of different aspects from various systems, doctrines or sources. By definition, an eclectic approach to coaching, or any other endeavor, fuses together components that were previously a part of another approach or theory. It is common for eclectic models of things to involve contradictory elements. An eclectic model of reading instruction might feature the contradictory elements of teaching students to carefully decode words, while also telling them to guess at unknown words to find one that "makes sense."

Eclectic models of coaching are widespread in our experiences within schools and districts. In one large school district we reviewed, eight individual coaches reported using coaching models that each had constructed independently based on what they knew and believed to be best. When the underlying philosophies were teased out of each, it became apparent that the district's approach to coaching, properly defined, was essentially an eclectic mix of the eclectic approaches adopted by their coaching team.

Agnostic Models Of Coaching

Our survey of approaches would be incomplete without including what we refer to as "agnostic" models of coaching. These are approaches that no one in the organization can explain in terms of their theoretical or philosophical basis. Consistent with agnosticism, practitioners of this approach frequently define their activities as a coach as consisting of "coaching". When asked to provide a philosophical rationale for their various activities, frequent rejoinders are, "because that just makes sense," or, similarly, "I think we have always done it this way."

We can now move to a side-by-side comparison of these approaches to Performance-Based Coaching™ to understand better how each responds to the eight -part test of coaching effectiveness established at the beginning of this chapter.

1. The change (adopting a new behavior) happens quickly.

2. The change is objectively measurable by others through visual or auditory information (see it or hear it).

3. The change is sustainable.

4. The change contributes to meeting an organizational goal.

5. The change is implemented system-wide.

6. The coach is highly skilled in the knowledge and behaviors they coach.

7. The cost of bringing about the change is organizationally feasible.

8. The value of the coach exceeds their cost to the organization.

Note: We are deliberately excluding from this analysis both eclectic and agnostic models of coaching due to the variances in their terms, practices and outcomes.

Characteristics of the Change	Performance-Based Coaching	Cognitive Coaching	Peer Coaching	Peer Observation and Assistance
Happens quickly	Yes	No	No	No
Objectively measurable by others	Yes	No	No	No
Sustainable	Yes	Sometimes	Sometimes	Sometimes
Contributes to meeting org. goals	Yes	Not always	Not always	Not always
System-wide	Yes	No	No	No
Coach is highly skilled	Yes	No	No	No
Feasible Cost	Yes	Sometimes	Usually Not	Usually Not
Coach adds value	Yes	Sometimes	Usually Not	Usually Not

You can see from the analysis above that there is a stark difference between coaching approaches. Probably the most salient difference between Performance-Based Coaching™ and the other approaches listed here is the unknowingness that is built into the non-performance-based approaches. In other words, the processes, goals, data and outcomes in the non-performance coaching approaches are highly idiosyncratic and largely subjective. Moreover, because the goal of these other approaches focuses so heavily on teacher comfort and "feelings" of improvement, system-wide impact is usually absent, since teachers and coaches could be working on things that have no relationship to school- or district-wide goals or initiatives. And because of the customized nature of the processes, it is difficult for both coaches, coachees and school and district leaders to understand beforehand – and frequently even during coaching – what the process is supposed to accomplish and whether it adds value to individuals or to the organization as a whole.

Trainer, Mentor, Peer, Expert Or Friend?

Remember back to the tennis story at the beginning of this chapter? Within its plot lies an analogy to perhaps the greatest myth and stumbling block to effective coaching in schools: the supposed stress and self-esteem risks related to helping teachers improve. Indeed, more coaching sessions are cancelled, coaches terminated, or coaching programs scratched before they ever start, because of a perception that helping someone to learn something new will be injurious to their identity, self-worth or public image. In few words, this is a fear manufactured and foisted upon teachers by unknowing and usually fearful people who are against improvement and definitely against opening classrooms to become a place for structured teacher learning.

But how can one be against improvement? Well, there are some people who hate Disneyland, so maybe this isn't so surprising. But if we agree that schools should be places where highly skilled teachers bring the best of what is known about teaching and learning to students, then the fear and destruction conjured up by these voices are smokescreens, usually for their own incompetence or for some political agenda they are advancing or defending.

Let's look further into the specific nature of the role between coach and teacher by revisiting briefly the story at the front of the chapter, and then by exploring the possible roles of a coach. You may recall that Daren, one of our aspiring tennis players, regularly looked to play people who were better than he was. Many of those adversaries were strangers. Some offered no verbal praise, while others took time to help Daren with strategy and techniques. As a group, the learning they imparted, in their own ways, was critical to his improvement. Karen, by contrast, played mostly with friends and lesser-skilled opponents. She grew to like their praise, her victories and the reassurance both of those provided. After a while the results of their tennis-improvement approaches looked like this:

- Daren was becoming an expert player, though he was not close friends with his "coaches".

- Karen's skills stayed about the same, and she had lots of friends to compliment her.

Recall that each of them wanted to be the best player on their respective teams. Neither of them set as their tennis-learning goal to make more friends. Paradoxically, Karen ended up an average player with a throng of friends and admirers. Daren ended up a top player in the league thanks in large part to the skillful play of superior opponents whom he viewed mainly as on-court acquaintances.

Establishing The Parameters

To be sure, the coaching role is a fluid one that requires tact, candor, expertise and professionalism. But it is critically important – especially in the early stages of a coaching relationship – that the coach establish the parameters of the coaching relationship. Many a coaching engagement has been spoiled by lack of role clarity on the part of both coach and teacher, so it is preferable to communicate and understand beforehand the nature and terms of the engagement. This follows logically from the fact that the primordial role of the coach is to assist a teacher to improve their performance in the classroom. That coaches and teachers may already know one another, or come to enjoy each other's company, is neither good nor bad. But at no point is the goal of coaching for coaches to be everyone's best friend. The misguided assumption that a coach must already have a good relationship with a teacher before coaching can begin is, of course, entirely fallacious. So too is the myth that the first several sessions, weeks or months, of a coach's job are to be consumed by "building" relationships with teachers in order to be able to coach them later.

In the real world, most of us are far more concerned that our doctor is an expert than whether we will become close friends, or that we knew her for several years before we decided to accept her expert advice as our doctor. What follows are five possible roles a coach could take, along with the pitfalls of each. As you will see, the role relationship between a coach and teacher sets the stage for rapid improvement, maintaining the status quo, or needless conflict and emotional drama, so understanding the implications of each of these is of great importance.

Trainer

In a strict sense, "training" is frequently associated with animals or sports. In education, we frequently refer to people as trainers, recognizing that their role is to impart information or procedures. In a coaching relationship, adopting a training stance tends to establish the time together as a one-way street: the trainer gives information and then leaves. For most kinds of coaching, with the possible exception of athletic coaching, it is more desirable to have interactions that utilize the experience and current skills of the teacher as well as the specialized knowledge and skills of the coach. At the end of the day, trainers deliver information and typically do not establish a mutual partnership that has as its goal learning a new behavior at a high level. In straight terms, trainers have no skin in the game.

Mentor

We find this word frequently used to describe the relationship between coaches and teachers. However, we are quick to disagree that such a relationship will support the requirements necessary for bringing about quick and lasting behavioral changes. Originating in Greek mythology, mentors are more like wise advisers from whom one seeks counsel prior to an action, or to fix something already broken. Like trainers, mentors dispense advice or opinions, but do not actively partner with their protégé to implement the recipe. Mentors also typically share their words of wisdom without witnessing or having first-hand knowledge of the context to which their sage advice may apply. And because advice is seen by the receiver as optional, it is easy to see why coaching relationships built on this role relationship frequently yield few results.

Peer

A standard dictionary tells us that a peer is someone of the same rank, value, quality, and ability. Coaching approaches, or theories based on such relationships, tend to be characterized by a focus on the aspects of the relationship more than the results of their work together. We saw in our tennis story that Karen played people of her own ability in her attempts to improve. But since they possessed the same level of competence, neither improved. The assertion that two non-experts working together can propel either or both of them to expert status is dubious at best and contradictory of most research on the topic. It also defies common sense and logic. Because both parties strive to be equal, the assessment of skills and outcomes is largely inaccurate because neither wants to offend the other. Still, this is a popular perspective since it focuses on affect and typically puts behavioral change in a distant back seat.

Friend

For a time in educational circles it was popular to speak of having "critical friends" to help one improve. But real-life experience for most of us has shown the inherent oxymoron in this term. The dualism and competing interests of being a friend and also helping someone to improve is a lot to manage during a 30-minute coaching session. If the goal is to implement something at a high level, that usually requires being able to discuss shortcomings, false assumptions, and mistakes, all of which are tough topics that can quickly strain a friendship. In short, friends are great to have, but when behavioral change is the goal, a more firm hand and the skills of a professional coach are more likely to prove advantageous.

Expert

Most of us seek expert assistance in areas of our lives where we know we lack the necessary experience, knowledge and skills. Rebuilding your car's transmission, filling a cavity, or preparing a complicated legal document are just a few examples of when we seek expert assistance. From these experts we have high expectations, and we place great faith – and money – in them to accomplish their tasks. The emotional security and confidence that comes from having an expert on the job also makes a huge difference. And so it is with coaching teachers to improve their performance. Teachers want and need to see their coach as an expert, someone whose knowledge and skills are up to the task at hand. For their part, Performance-Based Coaches™ have to be experts in all areas in which they coach; there are no exceptions to this. We get better by learning from and working with more competent others, and coaches carry a responsibility to their teachers to possess this expertise and professionalism.

Things To Ponder Or Discuss

1. Share a similar story of your own to the one about the tennis players that makes the same points?

2. Has your school or district ever produced or utilized a written description of the theory or philosophy that grounds the coaching approach you will use?

3. Is having a clear philosophical basis for the coaching approach in use really that important?

4. What explanation or hypotheses can you advance that would explain such a preoccupation with "affect" when it comes to helping teachers to do more things better more frequently with more students?

5. List the pros and cons of having a list of criteria like the one in this chapter to guide the selection of a coaching approach.

6. Do you agree that most of us gain security and confidence when we know we have an expert on our side?

7. Could a given coaching approach actually make teachers believe they are better than they really are?

The Coaches Corner

As described in this chapter, a great deal of consternation, worrying and lost time seems to be par for the course when it comes to defining a coach's role. In many – if not most – cases, no clear definition is ever formulated, leaving the coach and teachers to figure it out. This is unfortunate because it tends to destabilize both coaches and the teachers with whom they are supposed to work. If a coach is uncomfortable about establishing their role as an expert – or worse, does nothing to clarify their role – the coaching endeavor is usually doomed. After all, creating even more anxiety about coaching by vacillating about the role of the coach creates an initial lack of confidence by teachers in both the process and the players.

The question for you, coach, is how do you assess your current readiness to be a Performance-Based Coach™ and the expert status such a title and role connotes? Be as honest as possible when you do the following task to help you identify your current strengths and areas in need of improvement.

Draw a line down the middle of a piece of paper. List on the left side your strengths as a coach that show your teachers you are an expert in your field. Don't be shy and don't underrate yourself. Think broadly of the categories in which you have expertise.

On the right side of the paper, list three areas in which you need to improve in order to be viewed by your teachers as a true expert coach. Now you know what you need to work on.

The Leaders Lounge

Think about a speaker you have heard recently who was introduced in such a way that you were extremely excited to finally hear them talk.

Now think about a speaker you have heard recently whose introduction was so weak or non-existent that you started thinking about your to-do list before the speaker hit the podium. And so it is with your coach or coaches. Except this time, you are the Master of Ceremonies, and it is your express job, duty and privilege to introduce your coach or coaches to your staff. So how will you do this? Complete the exercise below to get a head start on making your teachers thrilled to begin working with your expert coaches.

For each coach, list the following on a piece of paper (yes, you must write them down):

1. What are three areas of knowledge they possess related to teaching and coaching that positions them above most other members of your staff?

2. What three behavioral aspects of their teaching record show that they were dynamite in the classroom when it came to student learning?

3. What are three specific elements of their personality that you believe uniquely qualify them for the coaching role?

4. Do they have specialized training or titles that convey expertise as coaches?

5. What gives you, as the leader of the organization, particular confidence that this is the right person for the job?

Tip: Remember, you have Alice, Biff and Carla listening to your presentation. Give them what they are listening for.

Now, put all this together into a nice package that rolls off your tongue and even makes you wish you could be a teacher to be coached by one of these experts. The initial consolidation of your coach's expertise is on you. Get it right and your organization's coaching program will get started with a great mix of enthusiasm, confidence and trust.

Fun Quiz

1. The story at the beginning of the chapter is used as a/n _____.
   a. metaphor
   b. simile
   c. analogy
   d. anecdote

2. The *Peer Coaching* approach involves _____ helping _____.
   a. teachers, students
   b. teachers, teachers
   c. coaches, teachers
   d. coaches, coaches

3. Which of the following is frequently the major concern of district officials when the topic of a coaching program comes up?
   a. credentials
   b. outcomes
   c. financial considerations
   d. time

4. The organizational value of an effective coach should be worth more than the total of their _____.
   a. experience
   b. training
   c. time on task
   d. compensation

5. Expert is to surgeon as conductor is to _____.
   a. audience
   b. orchestra
   c. music
   d. production

Chapter 5
Meet The Coaches

Introduction

This chapter marks an important turning point in our learning. The previous chapters have presented, explained and illustrated the knowledge vital to understanding human change and coaching in general. More specifically, we have presented the what and the why of Performance-Based Coaching™. The chapters that follow will synthesize this learning with new information about specific coaching methods and structures. These chapters serve to connect the "what" of Performance-Based Coaching™ to the "how". As we make this shift in focus to the practicum, it is important to remember that all of the content that came before this chapter, and all of the content still to come, hinges on one key precept, or principle.

- It is impossible to improve a school, but we can improve the behaviors of the people who work there.

Objectives

In this chapter you will learn:

1. How and why an average day of two coaches using different coaching approaches can be dramatically different and produce drastically different results;

2. Why the role of coach is a high turnover position in many schools and districts;

3. The proper role and responsibilities of a school or district leader in consolidating the authority, expertise and role of the coach;

4. To identify clearly why Performance-Based Coaching™ provides the most powerful structure and plan for changing teacher behaviors.

You've Probably Seen Or Heard This

Rosalina and Jennifer are both coaches who work at two different sites on opposite sides of the country. They have each been tasked with helping the teachers on their respective staffs to improve by participating in a coaching program that is new for both of the coaches and the schools to which they are assigned.

Our two coaches are similar in many ways as people and as professionals; they have both taught for more than six years, are viewed in their workplaces as excellent teachers, and both have young families at home. But with respect to their day-to-day routines as first-time coaches, they could not be any more dissimilar. Each of them is a site coach working within a coaching paradigm that is vastly different from the other. Rosalina works in a district that describes coaching as a "cognitive/affective collaborative relationship" similar to a coaching approach described earlier in this book. Jennifer's district is implementing a Performance-Based Coaching™ model. Though both would say that their goal is to help teachers to improve the quality of their instruction, how they were trained, their daily tasks and how they interact with teachers are substantially different.

The following are actual transcriptions of recorded interviews during one of our national Performance-Based Coaching Institutes™ where they discussed their training and preparation, daily tasks and how they interact with teachers.

Training And Preparation

Rosalina

Before I became a coach, I had always been a very good teacher, but I had always worked with students – never adults. I taught third and fourth grade, so I had experience with every subject area. I never really wanted to teach a lower grade and I definitely couldn't teach middle school. When the coaching position opened, our district director told me that I was recommended by my principal and that the district would provide all of the training that I needed. That summer before I started the new job was great! All of the new district coaches went to a three-day conference in Atlanta, Georgia, where we learned all about coaching. When we returned, the district director led two more days of training in our district boardroom. We practiced scripting videotaped lessons and role-played conversations we would have with our teachers about how to improve instruction. Everyone was so excited, and it was fun. I learned so much about how to build relationships with teachers and how to ask the right questions to get them thinking about instruction. Getting teachers to reflect on their practice was a main point of our training.

In July, we were sent to three different trainer-of-trainers sessions where we learned about our district's new math program, a positive behavior intervention system and about how to use one-to-one devices for the district's new focus on technology in the classroom. We were told that it would be our responsibility to train the teachers and help them implement the new programs that year.

About a week before school started, I moved from training at the district office to helping my principal prepare for the year at my school site. I helped create the master schedule, update the strategic plan, analyze student data and set goals for student performance. We had such a clear vision going into the year about what we wanted to accomplish. I couldn't wait for the teachers and the students to return.

At the first staff in-service, my principal, Mr. Diaz, introduced me. I remember him telling our staff that I would be a great support for them and that they could contact me for help if they needed it. I led a 15-minute team-building activity that helped me get to know the staff and what they saw as their strengths. Then Mr. Diaz reviewed the district's policies and procedures for site emergencies, absences and calling for a sub. At the end of the session, I walked the staff through all of the teacher editions and materials for the new math program that we would be rolling out during the year. I even organized the boxes and delivered them to the teachers so that they could have more time working in their classrooms.

Jennifer

I had coached my daughter's soccer team, but I had never been a coach before in a school setting. I had taught middle school language arts for honestly what seemed like an eternity – nine years to be exact. I was really good at it, but I was ready for a change, I mean, for a new challenge. When the announcement was posted for a K-8 site coach position at another school in our district, I thought it looked interesting, so I applied.

That summer was rough! Our district put together a week-long training program for the new coaches that took place during the district's summer school program. Every day, we spent the morning learning more about human change psychology than I could remember from college, then we learned about organizational change, coaching methods, how to allocate our time, and what our daily and weekly coaching schedules would look like. But that turned out to be the easy part! Every afternoon, the new coaches went into classrooms with an experienced coach. Sometimes, I would teach a lesson and I was coached in real-time exactly the same way I would be coaching our teachers. Other times, my coach would teach a lesson and I would have to coach him or her. If I missed an intervention opportunity, she always let me know, so I suppose she was still coaching me then, too.

As the week went on, we worked in classrooms with students of every grade level. I had never taught kindergarten, so that was very new for me – and a bit overwhelming. But the district coordinator and the consultants insisted that I have experience in as many settings as possible. Toward the end of the week, I began coaching teachers. My coach sat next to me, telling me when to jump in, what to say, and how to say it. All of this, our trainers told us, would ensure that our jobs as Performance-Based Coaches™ would begin successfully and be aligned with the goals of the district. It was a lot to understand and I was exhausted. I had also never learned so much or felt so prepared for anything.

At our first staff development session, Mr. Lemus, the site principal, talked about the coaching position, the role of the coach in promoting our school goals, and my background, for almost 15 minutes. He concluded by informing the staff that he and I would generate a coaching schedule and that coaching would begin on the third day of school. I spent another 30 minutes training the staff on the framework for a typical coaching cycle, and I explained what to expect when I enter the classroom. I also discussed the purpose and benefits of Performance-Based Coaching™ and its rationale.

The staff had lots of questions about coaching, particularly about how coaching objectives would be established. Mr. Lemus reiterated that all coaching sessions would be driven by observable data, and that most teachers would be working with me on three specific teaching behaviors that had been established by the district. I won't say that everyone was excited at first, but it was nice to hear after the presentation from several teachers that they had a much better understanding of what coaching was supposed to accomplish.

Training and Preparation at a Glance	
Rosalina	Jennifer
Off-campus seminar-style training was provided	On-site seminar and in-class practicum training were provided
Minimal focus on psychology or organizational change No additional experience in grade levels or subject areas was encouraged prior to coaching	Heavy grounding in individual psychology and how that affects change; emphasis on how organizations change
Discussion and role-play were the focus of district trainings	Experience across all grades and content areas was required and provided prior to coaching
Staff was introduced to the coach at the beginning of the year	Actual use of coaching methods was the focus of district trainings
	Staff was informed about expectations and the goals of coaching at the beginning of the year

Daily Responsibilities

Rosalina

On a daily basis, I wear so many hats. It really depends on the day. Teachers don't usually like me to come into their rooms on Mondays, so I usually spend time planning and preparing for the weekly after-school staff development session I conduct. My principal is usually at the district office on Mondays, so I also help out with discipline in the office until he returns. On Tuesdays, I lead the grade-level data meetings where we look at data points from recent benchmark assessments and discuss how we can increase student performance. On Wednesdays, I try to get into a few classrooms to observe, but I also have to pull reading intervention groups to help teachers with their tier three interventions. On Thursdays, I sit in on IEP or evaluation team meetings so that I can provide suggestions to teachers and help them support the students who are struggling. Fridays are another no-go for coaching, so I pull math intervention groups and schedule debrief conversations for the teachers that I observed earlier in the week. Sometimes, I also help with grant writing and anything else that my principal needs help with during the week. If teachers sign up for coaching, I'll always make time to go in and observe or schedule a time to cover their class so that they can observe one of their peers. But that all depends on the week and if I can fit it in.

Jennifer

Well, my first week went pretty much like my 20th week, which makes it sound like I do the same thing every day. But since I work with eight teachers at a time — each on a three-week cycle — and they are all at various places in their progression, the methods I use and the behaviors that we target during their coaching sessions end up giving me a pretty full and varied day. Once a week I lead a staff development session after school, so I reserve one morning a week for the planning and preparation of that training. I also conference with Mr. Lemus on Monday mornings to review the prior week's work and to set the teacher objectives for the coming week. I also meet monthly at various sites with the other site coaches, the district coordinator and an external consultant for continued coach development training. Just like my initial summer training, those are usually half-day meetings where we go further in depth on the coaching methods and the psychology behind what we do. Then we go into classrooms and take turns coaching, and then the other coaches and the consultant coach us.

Every day, I have between four and six 45-minute in-class coaching sessions where I work side-by-side with teachers and their students. We target one behavior at a time and work together to improve the teacher's use of that behavior.

Daily Schedule at a Glance	
Rosalina	Jennifer
Constantly varied schedule	Consistent schedule
Most time is spent out of classrooms	Most time is spent in classrooms
Several impromptu observations each week	Four to six coaching sessions per day
Content of coaching is not clear	Specific behavioral objectives drive all coaching sessions
Principal is rarely involved or aware of in-class work	Principal and coach meet regularly to plan the future, analyze the past

Teacher Interaction

Rosalina

When I enter a classroom, I always take my blue or my red clipboard. The blue one tells the teachers that I am watching for student engagement and classroom management. When I have the red clipboard, I am watching for objectives and teacher questioning. I have a checklist of indicators that I have provided to the teachers. Sometimes, I will also script some of the lesson or take notes. I also like to quietly ask some of the students about what they are learning so that I can tell the teacher what they said. I sit at the back of the room for between five and 10 minutes before writing a brief note to leave on the teacher's desk. I like to tell them one thing that they were doing well, but I also usually leave them a suggestion to improve the lesson or maybe a reminder about something. Then I try to get to as many classrooms as I can before I need to pull a small of students for intervention instruction.

After the observations, teachers know that if they have questions about my note they can email me any time. If I was concerned about anything that I saw during my observations, I'll schedule a meeting with the teacher to talk about the lesson. Sometimes, it takes a couple of days for our schedules to align, but we can usually figure out a time to meet that week. When we meet, I ask questions to get them thinking about how they might do the lesson differently in the future. I also try to generate reflective questions that cause them to analyze their own teaching. If the lesson happened that day, we can usually have a good conversation. If it has been a few days, I try my best to remind the teacher about what I saw as we talk so that they can remember. I usually schedule a follow-up observation for after the meeting if the teacher wants more support or if they are currently working on a performance plan with the site principal.

I always want them to know when I am coming so it isn't a surprise or a "gotcha". It's important for them to feel comfortable with the process. Honestly, the hardest part is the scheduling. It is just hard to find the time to fit it all in and the teachers are usually not too excited to give up a prep period or meet outside of the school day. I do the best that I can.

Jennifer

I don't always schedule the exact time for each coaching session with the teachers on my cycle. If the behavior we are targeting is content specific, I make sure to arrive during their designated time for that subject area, but they know that I may drop in really at any time during the day if we are working together in a coaching cycle. That way, if a teacher is out sick, I can use their scheduled time to support another teacher instead of losing the time altogether.

I try my best when entering the classroom to cause as little interruption as possible. I don't talk to the students or interrupt the lesson. I grab a chair near the front of the room and quietly sit down to give the teacher my full attention. Students are pretty much used to me being there, so things keep going. Depending on the coaching method, I may demonstrate a portion of the lesson, we might teach together, or I may provide real-time feedback on the lesson. During a 45-minute coaching session, I would say that I interact verbally with most teachers approximately every three to four minutes. Usually, I address my comments to a teacher in a whisper voice, or hand them a sticky note with a question they should ask. With some teachers, we actually have a kind of on-going conversation throughout the lesson, which really seems to engage the students as well.

At the end of the session, usually during the independent practice phase of the teacher's lesson, I pull the teacher aside to briefly summarize our focus and let them ask me specific questions. On my way out, I leave a physical representation — usually a small sign on the back wall or door — that reminds the teacher of the behavior that we focused on.

The teachers can contact me after each session if they want to talk further, but as I am in their rooms approximately five times during their three-week cycle, we can usually fit everything in during each session. Teachers really appreciate not having to give up time outside of class and it helps me schedule more sessions.

Teacher Interaction at a Glance	
Rosalina	Jennifer
Observations are usually always scheduled	Coaching sessions can occur at any time of day during a cycle
Checklists and notes are utilized	Real-time feedback is provided
Positive comments are left behind	Teacher and coach analyze and discuss progress toward the coaching goal as students do independent work
Observations are inconsistently timed	Observations occur consistently during a three-week cycle
Other non-coaching duties frequently interrupt the coach's schedule	The majority of the coach's day is spent in classrooms helping teachers

Summary

Rosalina

I have never been so busy. It feels like every year there is more to do. I have built such great relationships on my campus and I am glad that I can help teachers and students. I just wish that I had more time and I wish more teachers wanted coaching.

Jennifer

Of course, not everyone loves this type of coaching. I have two teachers in particular who would much rather go back to being left alone to teach, but we have grown to respect each other and the role we each play in improving student achievement. They seem to understand that this is a high priority for the school and for Mr. Lemus, so they do their part. Overall, my job as a coach is even more structured than when I was teaching eighth-grade ELA, but it is rarely boring. Now, everybody understands how coaching works and what we are trying to accomplish with it; just that makes my job a lot more efficient. The best part for me is walking out of a classroom having seen a teacher doing something consistently that they were not doing before our cycle began. That's very rewarding.

Things To Ponder Or Discuss

1. What questions would you ask Rosalina and/or Jennifer based on what they have shared here?

2. Which of these approaches to coaching do you think the majority of your current site's teaching staff would prefer?

3. What role should return on public funds, i.e., grant money and other funding sources, play in the selection and implementation of a coaching model and program?

4. Is there a "right" or "best" type of personality to be a coach?

5. Why would a school leader support or not support a school-wide coaching program?

The Coaches Corner

How much of yourself and your experiences as a coach do you see in these testimonies?

Is there some aspect of either Rosalina's or Jennifer's narrative that particularly resonates with you?

Which of these better exemplifies what you would want in a coach if you were a teacher?

If you were investing your own money in a coaching program, which of the two models presented here would you feel most confident in for bringing about a school- or system-wide change?

The Leaders Lounge

Clearly, a skilled coach working within a well-designed structure holds tremendous promise for improving teachers' instructional practices. That said, a coach is just one part — albeit an important part — of a comprehensive system for improvement. A key question for leaders to frequently consider is this:

> *What percentage of the success of a school-wide coaching effort are you willing to take responsibility for?*

This is a tough question that forces leaders to prioritize, analyze and to take ownership. It also puts forth the assertion that leadership proceeds ahead of the coach. Coaches cannot both lead and execute their tasks simultaneously, though many are erroneously asked to do just that.

Now, identify other factors critical to the success of your site's or district's coaching program. For example, if other factors like district-organized trainings, adequate budget and teacher buy-in are important, what impact does each of these have in percentage terms to the total impact and efficacy of coaching?

When you are done with this exercise, you should have a list of factors, beginning with yourself. Next to each factor is a percentage amount that corresponds to its impact on the success of your coaching effort. All of your percentages should sum to 100.

Put this list in a visible place and review it often. You may not be able to control all of the factors, but you can control your own impact, which is why you are at the top of the list.

Fun Quiz

1. The biggest non-recurring resource for a coach is _____.
   a. time
   b. money
   c. supplies
   d. principal support

2. What is the approximate percentage of time Rosalina spends in class actually coaching teachers during a typical week?
   a. less than 10 percent
   b. 10-25 percent
   c. 26-50 percent
   d. more than 50 percent

3. Leaving a note on a teacher's desk with a couple positive comments and one suggestion for improvement is known as _____.
   a. selective reinforcement
   b. engagement
   c. sandwiching
   d. feedback

4. When site or district leaders' descriptions of coaching are different than what coaches say, teachers receive a _____ _____.
   a. big headache
   b. free pass
   c. strange illusion
   d. mixed message

5. Coaches are responsible for scheduling and allocating their time each week.

   Agree   Disagree   Not Sure

Chapter 6
The Performance-Based Coaching Cycle

Introduction

Philosophical frameworks for humans helping other humans to do something better have both existed and been debated since the days when the Greek philosophers Socrates, Plato and Aristotle attempted to explain how a person might become the best version of him or herself. Though they disagreed on plenty, these titans of ancient philosophy all endorsed a central principle. Namely, that humans are forgetful, habit-based organisms that can only truly change if they consistently practice doing things in real-life situations that differ from their ingrained habits. Translated into common speech, these philosophers agreed that people are capable of changing their deep-rooted and long-enduring patterns of how they think, feel and behave.

Even today, human change theories are hotly debated, as are ideas about how a theory and approach to "coaching" fit into the total human improvement equation. Indeed, the idea that coaching has a role to play in human change brings about even more questions. What makes a good coach? What should be the relationship between a coach and his/her *coachee*? What is the role of the coach during the coaching process? Depending on who you ask, these questions can yield drastically different answers, deriving largely from the philosophical or theoretical orientation held by the respondent. Ask a dozen coaches this question: what is the primary outcome of your work? You would probably be surprised — or not — by the divergence of answers.

As you have learned throughout this book, Performance-Based Coaching™ differs from other approaches by prioritizing a change in behavior as the first and most important aspect of both the coaching process and its intended outcome. When we establish behavior as the primary metric of improvement, a new and more compelling set of questions emerges. How do we accelerate the change process? How does a coach ensure immediate and consistent implementation of new skills? How do we coach in ways that build sustainability of new behaviors? What will happen to the behavior after the coaching relationship is ended? These are the questions that guide a Performance-Based Coach™. These are the questions we will begin to answer in this chapter.

Objectives

In this chapter you will learn:

1. Why specificity of terms and language is critical to establishing maximum outcomes from coaching;
2. What is a coaching cycle;
3. The characteristics of effective coaching goals;

4. The role of a Performance-Based Coach™ for each component of the coaching cycle.

You've Probably Seen Or Heard This Before

It's almost 2:00 pm on a Wednesday and a third-grade teaching team at Maryland Elementary School in the heart of New Mexico is meeting with their site reading coach to discuss student data with the goal of improving student achievement. They look at the computer screen in front of the room to see an all-too-familiar bar graph showing the number of students in each classroom that have met, approached or fallen below the standard on a recent benchmark assessment.

Mrs. Johnston, a 15-year teaching veteran, sighs and says, "We spent a lot of time on this. The test just asked things differently. It was confusing to the students." The rest of the team around the table nods in agreement.

Their school coach, Ms. Teal, interjects. "I understand the frustration. How can we help the students do better in the future?"

"Let's just look and see how it's going to be asked next time," suggests Mr. Butler. "Then we can make sure to write some questions like that for the students to practice."

Mrs. Johnston scoffs. "We have done that already. The next test won't ask it the same way."

Ms. Teal interjects again and asks Sally, a teacher new to the school the previous year, an interesting question. "Sally, your students did quite well on this standard. What did you do?"

Sally, the team's newest teacher, somewhat hesitantly responds. "I taught the students how to solve the problem and then they used their laptops to practice solving similar problems while I pulled small groups to help the students who were struggling." A low, rolling groan can be heard around the table. Then each team member, in turn, informs the group that what was just described is similar to what they also currently do or to something that they have tried in the past without success.

Ms. Teal supportively adds, "I've seen you do your small-group work a certain way Sally and it was very effective. Can we all agree to try it like this starting next week? Let me know when you think you will try it out and I'll come in and observe." As the teachers take turns signing up for an observation time, they rush out of the room to get their students ready for dismissal.

The Well-Intentioned Plan That Omits Behavior

Coaches across the country are asked to lead meetings just like this where some form of data is expected to yield a group commitment to change. But just like at the Maryland School meeting from our scenario, the meetings frequently yield yet another educational paradox: the creation of a plan that yields no, or very little, change in behavior. The format (in many places, this is almost like a script) for this predictable outcome goes as follows: various practices are shared, with each usually bearing the support of its sponsor. Members politely listen, nod and then share their practice. Each teacher presents his or her way as meritorious in some way or other. Someone, usually a coach, asks that they all try something and the meeting adjourns. Most go back to their status quo. And so it goes.

Freeform discussions where teachers talk with each other about what led to greater achievement among their students is similar to having a group of mothers talk about what practices keep their children from catching the flu. Many mothers would share similar practices such as diet, exercise, or bathing routines, but most would quickly agree that they "already do those things". This leaves two possible outcomes for the discussion: everyone leaves the gathering with little thought given to a behavioral change that differs from their norm, or some of the group members decide to give a new idea a whirl. Imagine one mother in the group sharing her practice of rubbing peppermint oil on her son's feet at night to prevent the flu. That night, there is a rush on peppermint oil at the store, but many of the children still catch the flu regardless of the intervention.

This tendency of a few to try something new based only on a limited endorsement by another often happens when one teacher convincingly shares a unique app, hot tip or internet resource. The other team members are quick to purchase the magic bullet only to find that the outcomes stayed the same. The teacher who was effective before is still effective with the new app. The teachers who struggled before now struggle with the new app or resource.

When this cycle of teacher meetings was raised with Ms. Teal and her principal at Maryland Elementary School as a possible explanation for why teacher change happened only occasionally and with a few teachers, she offered the following information.

> *I am in classrooms all the time. I know that all of the teachers teach with similar lessons and materials because they plan together. What they don't realize is how differently each of them actually implements the plans that they have made. We spend so much time talking about instruction, but at the end of the year, most of my teachers are still teaching the same way they always have. When scores come out, if they aren't positive outcomes, I am also quick to be blamed as people often say that they did exactly what I told them to do in our meetings. It is so frustrating.*

Performance: The Coach's Singular Focus

At the risk of understatement, the change process –as we have learned — isn't easy. It is a complex process that requires time, commitment and consistency for everyone involved. Changing behaviors isn't something we can easily achieve through an observation and quick discussion that glosses over the background assumptions, beliefs and experiences that led to the practices currently in place. In fact, to change teacher behavior in a way that will yield greater student achievement requires coaches to *D.I.G.* into the process.

This simple acronym will help us to remember the three parts of what we refer to as the Performance-Based Coaching Cycle™, which is easily defined as the major activities that happen between a coach and a teacher during a given period of time.

D.I.G.

> D: Define
> I: Intervene
> G: Generalize

Each letter of the acronym represents a major component of the Performance-Based Coaching Cycle™. Before we elaborate on each of these components, it's helpful to visualize each of them as a spoke on a wheel that is in constant spinning motion. At any given time, the coach and teacher may be at a single place on the wheel or dealing with multiple components of the wheel. The following diagram may help.

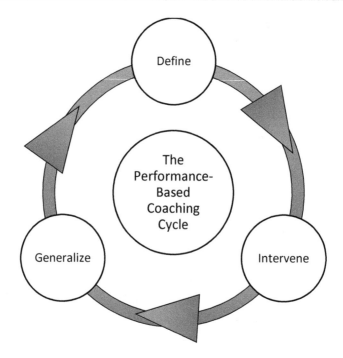

At this point in our discussion a logical question is, "How long is a typical coaching cycle?" We find that coaching cycles that last between four and six weeks to be maximally effective. During this time period, most Performance-Based Coaches™ are able to work with five to six teachers. This maximizes the time a coach spends with each teacher and gives them enough total time to focus and work on the coaching goal for that cycle. It is usually the case that a teacher on a 25-member faculty would be party to a coaching cycle at least twice a year or more, depending on factors specific to each teacher, coach and the school or district. Now let's look at the three parts of a coaching cycle.

D = Define

Sadly, most attempts at coaching fail before they even truly begin. They fail at the point when a coach begins to speak, and the teacher attempts to listen. This can actually be the most frustrating aspect of coaching to both parties and detrimental to the process, even though both parties have the best intentions. To better understand why this first attempt at communication regarding a change can sour quickly, we must recall some of the typical professional development practices that we discussed earlier, and how those can affect a teacher's view of their own learning and that of the organization. For example, in order to save money and to build "capacity," thousands of teachers have been sent to one-and-two-day seminars to learn about topics like "student engagement," "instructional rigor," "differentiation" and "student inquiry." It is common for teachers who attend these trainings to be asked, upon their return to campus, to "train" their peers or share what they learned. The invitation and format for this may sound familiar to you. "Sheila and Mike," says the principal, "please take the last 25 minutes of our staff meeting to teach everyone what you learned at the two-day seminar on vocabulary building." That is quite a task.

What ensues next is a professional version of "The Telephone Game". Crammed into a tight time spot, Sheila and Mike generalize, then generalize, and then generalize some more while the clock speeds toward their metaphorical version of Cinderella's midnight curfew. With no time to adequately define terms or processes, their presentation lacks specificity, theoretical foundation, and detailed descriptions of the how and why of what they learned. The audience — teachers who have heard these types of truncated presentations before — knows to expect generalities, underdeveloped descriptions and vague terminology. In short, everything about the presentation — through no deliberate fault of Mike or Sheila — is blurry, largely because of the linguistic vagary typical of so many educational presentations.

As a result, two things happen. Most everyone concludes that they are already doing something like what Mike and Sheila described. Second, terms are not defined, or they are defined so sloppily, that everyone is allowed to utilize their own meanings. Played out fully, all in attendance agree that they agree on the meanings of terms without ever having to compare meanings or arrive at universally understood meanings. This self-perpetuating cycle creates the very first steep hill for a coach to climb.

Because terms are rarely defined and agreed upon in public education settings, educators come to tolerate –and frequently promote — a vast array of different definitions and understandings of the terms, concepts and practices related to teaching and learning. It is all too common for a teacher, coach, administrator or consultant to observe a classroom in action and blithely conclude that the teacher needs "to increase the rigor" of instruction, or that the lesson "lacked focus." Given the non-agreed-upon meanings of the terms, the classroom teacher is quick to disagree, arguing that the lesson was a model of "rigor" and "focus". Seeking to calm the waters, the site principal opines that, for him, the lesson was "pretty rigorous for the most part, and it seemed pretty focused to me." And so it goes.

Another challenge of the *Define* phase of The Performance-Based Coaching Cycle™ is when all terms used relate to processes or products rather than to behaviors. (It may be helpful to read the previous sentence again. We are swinging open a big door here.) For example, who is against *student engagement*? Is anyone anti-*meaningful instruction*? Is there a teacher in the land who is diametrically opposed to *maximizing learning*? When we accept these terms as solely representative of processes or of final products, we have sidestepped the role of specific human behaviors in bringing about an improvement in student learning. As coaches, we have to define, in behavioral terms, what we want to see teachers doing or saying. What are the five specific teacher behaviors that show us "maximizing learning"? What are three specific student behaviors that would show us "student engagement"? As a fun and enlightening game, think for a moment of all the terms bandied about during a single staff meeting, a short in-service training, or a university education class. Notice how the terms used are simply left open. Notice how the terms are accepted on their face value and then used again and again as if everyone is in universal agreement. This is one of the many challenges coaches are up against and is why defining terms is the foyer of Performance-Based Coaching™.

We begin a coaching cycle by digging into the definitions of terms, usually beginning with the teacher behaviors we want to be able to see and hear. We sometimes are inclusive of student behaviors as well if those behaviors derive from a particular teacher behavior. This means working hard to establish terms that are mutually understood and that have as little vagary or wiggle room as possible. It may be helpful to define the word *behavior* itself, since it is frequently equated with thinking, intent, or desire. Behavior is best defined as an action that can either be seen or heard. You will learn more later in this book about how to identify evidence of behaviors by looking for, collecting and analyzing visual or audio evidence.

Deconstructing Processes And Products

A big element of this phase of a coaching cycle is deconstructing a common (and usually undefined) term into its constituent behavioral elements. This is a task that gets better with practice. Let's look at an example. Say a school site goal is to "maximize instructional minutes." Though it sounds admirable and worthy, in this form it is not a goal that a Performance-Based Coach™ can use to work effectively with a teacher. Why? Based on our previous discussion, this term is both a process and a product, neither of which let us know the teacher behaviors necessary. Second, the term is meaningless, or poly-meaningful, if left alone. It can mean whatever you or I want it to mean or need it to mean. Our task is to break it down into behavioral terms; if a teacher does behavior X, then instructional minutes are maximized. If we see or hear evidence during instruction of five identified behaviors, then we can say that instructional minutes are being maximized.

Our analysis might look like this.

Site Goal: Maximization Of Instructional Minutes
Observable Teacher Behaviors

Indicator	Visible	Audible
Teacher starts lesson on time		
Teacher follows time allotments from lesson plan		
Teacher ends lesson on time		
Teacher identifies time allocations for tasks		
Teacher's rate of speech is constant, with no rapid spurts to make up time		
Teacher programs specific time to help struggling students		
Teacher language is solely about the instructional content		
Teacher has instructional materials ready for student use		
Teacher provides specific time allotment for students to prepare for lesson		
Teacher discourages student responses that are off-task		

By designing a list like this, coaches are essentially developing a list of coaching goals for teachers. A coach could further re-order the list based on individual teacher skills, such that coaching proceeds along a hierarchy of behaviors. Not surprisingly, this type of analysis is usually brand new for most educators, but it serves to emphatically declare that specific definitions will be the rule henceforth.

To foreshadow what is to follow later, it may be helpful to see how this emphasis on behavior further defines our model of coaching.

Here are four ways a focus on behavior transforms coaching, even in the earliest stages of working with a teacher when you are digging into terms and definitions.

1. List the observable or audible behaviors that are present during a lesson that either advance or impede student learning.

2. Describe in detail the desired behavior. What will it look like? What will it sound like?

3. Describe the differences between the behaviors that are currently being observed in the classroom with those behaviors that are needed to improve student learning.

4. Measure how often the currently observed behaviors are occurring and set a goal for how often a more effective behavior is expected.

As you can see, digging into terms and definitions early helps everyone involved in coaching to understand the lay of the land. Defining terms in behavioral parlance takes work, patience and a willingness to parse. Instead of talking with a teacher about "maximizing instructional time", the conversation is one of identifying behaviors that indeed maximize time. If we want students to use academic words in their oral answers, what specific student behaviors would manifest visual or audible proof of that? What specific teacher behaviors get students to craft academic-sounding oral sentences?

I: Intervene

Now that the coach and the teacher have clearly defined the behavior or behaviors that will be the focus of our coaching cycle, the process of change now requires *intervention* from the coach. At this point, the teacher knows their behavioral goal. They know exactly what it is that they need to learn to do to increase student achievement. But as we know, learning, applying and mastering a new behavior is tough to pull off by yourself. Incorporating a new behavior — and usually one that feels initially uncomfortable — is accelerated when a teacher is pushed to work successfully with support at a level they would not be able to do independently. This support can take many forms, all of which you will learn in the subsequent chapters on coaching methods. Thinking about *learning* this way — that it frequently requires a well-meaning push — means that we can't expect teachers to improve their practice simply by observing them for previously demanded requirements. And neither does it mean that by having them observe someone more expert will they appropriate those talents.

By eschewing the traditional practice of simply observing teachers in favor of intervening to help them learn something new, we have turned most coaching practices on their head. For this reason, Performance-Based Coaches™ spend the great majority of their time in classrooms helping teachers to learn new behaviors. We should note here that the word *intervention* (and its derivative, *to intervene*) should not have any negative connotations, since it simply means that the coach will "step into" instruction to provide direct verbal and behavioral support to the teacher (see how we are defining terms?). This focus on intervention creates the conditions under which a teacher can successfully practice new behaviors and form new habits with the collaboration of an expert coach. Asking teachers to try something new or different without support is to replicate the failed cycle of "monastic" learning we detailed at the outset of this book.

Intervening does not mean leaving notes for teachers to consider in hindsight, nor does it mean proffering a quick hot tip, or having subjunctive discussions about the lesson after school ("What would you have done differently if you had gained a Ph.D. in small-group instruction before teaching this lesson?"). To intervene, coaches must skillfully rely on all or some combination of the following coach behaviors:

1. Demonstrate the exact behavior that is the focus of the coaching cycle in the teacher's own classroom with the teacher's own students.

2. Step-in to the lesson when the desired behavior doesn't occur in order to provide a clear and actionable directive or example to the teacher as to what he/she needs to do next.

3. Re-direct the teacher to practice the desired behavior when they forget to use it.

G: Generalize

Do students behave the same way in the classroom as on the playground? Do they behave the same way on a rainy day as they do on a sunny day? Do students behave the same way with a substitute as with their regular teacher? The answer to all of these is "Of course not!" So too, it is true that a teacher does not behave the same way during all of their teaching day, for each of their subjects, with every student or on the day before a vacation. This is the ultimate frustration for coaches and teachers alike in many coaching systems. A teacher is given a new tool or implements a type of instruction during one part of the day but struggles to implement that same method or behavior at other times. We see this often with teachers who can, for example, effectively utilize small reading groups in the morning but who are unable to utilize the same small group instructional practice during math, science, or writing. Coaching is only as effective as the teacher's ability to generalize new and more effective target behaviors to all aspects of their teaching. To generalize, coaches must help teachers by:

1. Co-planning with them for the implementation of newly learned and practiced target behaviors into different subject areas and periods of the instructional day.

2. Dropping-in during different instructional periods to coach extemporaneously throughout the coaching cycle.

3. Set goals for future coaching cycles that build directly upon the current cycle's targeted behavior or behaviors.

It is a common myth that people will automatically generalize the use of a new behavior across different contexts. What is more true is that our hyper focus on the new behavior usually comes within a specific context where we practice and learn to incorporate it. Moving that behavior to a new place, with different people, or under different conditions is sometimes viewed as almost a new and separate task. Eating healthy foods, for example, comprises an array of behaviors that are sometimes easier to learn and practice when all foods are purchased for their healthy quality and meals are prepared at home. But going to a restaurant, on vacation, or to a family potluck or barbecue can throw a monkey wrench into our goal of generalizing our healthy-eating behaviors to outside the home. Generalizing a behavior to a new setting frequently needs a coach's support before we can say that a teacher has achieved sustainability with a particular behavior.

You will learn in a subsequent chapter how to design and implement a maximally effective coaching cycle that combines what you have learned about *D.I.G.* with specific coaching methods for bringing about rapid, effective and sustainable changes in teacher performance.

Things To Ponder Or Discuss

1. What are some of the educational terms that are often tossed around in meetings without clearly defining them? How might their various interpretations explain instructional variance across classrooms and grade levels?

2. How do we decide if one practice is more effective than another? If the practice is more effective, how often should it be used? What or who is the arbiter of what makes something "effective"?

3. In the past, how often have you been asked to implement a new skill without further support in your own classroom? How have subsequent demands or initiatives built upon those skills or contradicted them?

4. Do teachers generally struggle to implement effective practices across all periods or subject areas?

5. Do teachers (or people) need help to discard old practices that are no longer effective for the current context of their work (or life)?

6. On the "Wow, that is strange!" scale, how did you react to learning about the Performance-Based Coaching™ practices of defining terms, and intervening in a teacher's lesson in real time?

The Coaches Corner

Some of us enjoy word games; others don't. But a central part of executing well the tasks of a Performance-Based Coach™, as you learned in this chapter, is being as specific as possible in all of your language use. Indeed, we can say that accuracy of communication by a coach begets increased accuracy of language use by teachers and other educators. Unfortunately, you probably have much experience in education similar to the examples used in this chapter; a free-for-all of terms and language structures that mainly serve to help people think they are actually talking about and doing the same things. Your leadership role in the area of language clarity is essential for the teachers and other educators with whom you interact, though we agree it can be some heavy lifting. Here is a simple way for you to think about your communication with teachers, administrators and others.

A Is For Accuracy

Is the language you use a model of accuracy? Do you define terms and use grammar reflective of a high level of competence and correctness? Are your sentences free of educational mumbo jumbo, jargon and catch phrases? Are your written communications spelled and punctuated correctly so that you are representing yourself and your important position as coach as professionally as possible?

B Is For Brevity

If something can be said with 10 words, why use 20 words? We sometimes believe that the use of more words, crammed ever more tightly together and sprinkled with abundant pauses, inflections, facial expressions and subordinations, actually helps most people to understand our intended message. Your time as a coach is valuable, as is that of your teachers. Keep your language brief and to the point. This is sage advice for all of your communications, whether aloud or in writing.

C Is For Clarity

One dictionary definition for the word *clear* is "free from clouds or mist". Though it seemingly refers to weather conditions, we might generalize it to our communications as coaches. Are your messages and information easily understandable, free of clouds or mist? Do teachers, through their verbal responses, indicate that you are being understood? If you find yourself asking teachers, "Do you know what I mean?" you may want to work on your clarity. It is not only a sign of a sharp mind, but also sharpens the minds of others.

The Leaders Lounge

As you may have deduced from the information in this chapter about coaching cycles, they involve quite a bit of cognitive, affective and behavioral work on the part of your coach or coaches. You can lighten their burden as they initiate and manage these coaching cycles by assuming responsibility and accountability for three major logistical requirements.

1. Announce and distribute the weekly schedules of your coach or coaches.

    Your coach is probably in the best position to draw up a weekly schedule, together with your input. After a short time, schedules can be fairly generic and require just the rotation of teachers through them. But your coach needs you to consolidate the authority of the schedule by its announcement and distribution by you. You as site leader are telling the staff that they will put their assigned time slot on their calendars and that you will monitor their compliance with adhering to the schedule.

2. Establish regular written updates from you that directly address the benefits of coaching.

In five minutes, you can probably come up with 10 good things about coaching, even if they have yet to actually happen. These are benefits. They are not goals, objectives, hopes or dreams. They're just good things for your teachers, your students and for your school that are possible through coaching. Share, in writing, one of these every two weeks; not the whole list, just one. People buy laundry soap because of its benefits. No one cares about its chemical makeup. You are the key spokesperson at your site for the benefits of coaching.

3. Make it a point to regularly tell individuals about recent instructional improvements that are due to your coaching program.

Individuals love to hear that you noticed they have improved. Break all of the rules you have been erroneously taught about not naming individuals in favor of rewarding groups (even though everyone knows not everyone in the group deserves reward). Identify teachers who are meeting — or have met — their coaching goals by name. Do it loud and proud, even in front of others. They will go home and tell five people about your praise and the benefits of your coaching program. Guaranteed.

Fun Quiz

1. When describing desired behaviors that are the target of a coaching cycle, we focus on audible and _____ indicators to measure implementation.
   a. affective
   b. checklists of
   c. visible
   d. audio

2. Definition is to terms as ingredients are to _____.
   a. cakes
   b. recipe
   c. cooking
   d. inputs

3. Coaching sessions are scheduled in advance so that teachers can prepare for their lessons.
   a. always
   b. sometimes
   c. never

4. Having teachers observe their peers is an effective way to improve instruction.
   a. true
   b. false
   c. not sure

5. Teachers should focus on one subject or class period to practice their new skills.
   a. true
   b. false
   c. not sure

Chapter 7
The Methods Of Performance-Based Coaching
Part One

Introduction

Finally, we have arrived at the actual methods of Performance-Based Coaching™ you will use with your teachers to bring about fast, effective and sustainable new behaviors. A good question you may be asking is, "Why didn't these methods come earlier in the book?" You probably know the answer by now. Performance-Based Coaching™ is itself a unified theory and set of principles and practices related to the science and art of teacher improvement. Unlike so many "innovations" in education that are billed as "easy" and "quick-fixes" to an enduring problem, the methods that you are about to learn and practice have a deep and sturdy foundation across a variety of disciplines, most notably the behavioral sciences (i.e., psychology, sociology and even economics), and science and mathematics (everything is observable and measurable). This chapter introduces you to the first three methods of Performance-

Based Coaching™. You will quickly see that each method is defined by a set of procedural steps designed to accomplish a specific purpose. These first three methods are grouped together because they typically occur toward the beginning of a coaching cycle and they have many coaching behaviors in common.

Objectives

In this chapter you will learn:

1. The first three coaching methods, their steps and their actual use;

2. That the focus of each method is different, but all focus on helping a teacher to implement or enhance the use of a new behavior;

3. That each method serves the established behavioral goal or goals for a teacher during a given coaching cycle;

4. Why observable change or improvement should be the planned outcome for each coaching session.

You've Probably Seen Or Heard This Before

Have you ever caught yourself breathing heavily after climbing a flight of stairs, not been happy with something that you saw in the mirror, or maybe just decided that you wanted to be healthier? If you are anything like Mrs. Schmidt, a middle school math coach in Houston, Texas, you have not only felt this way once, but probably multiple times throughout your life. We met Mrs. Smith during a coach training program where, as a prelude to analyzing teacher coaching, we were discussing personal changes that we had either successfully achieved or failed to realize. Her story resonated with most of us.

I had tried to get in shape for years! You all know what I mean. I had extra weight. I was always tired, and I never felt good. I tried everything. Well, I guess I should say that I bought everything. First, it was those workout DVDs, then it was a treadmill, and after that it was an ab cruncher. I used them every day. Sometimes, I would even get frustrated and use them twice a day, but the small changes would quickly disappear, and I would be back to step one. After each failure I would blame the program and felt like I had wasted my time and money.

Finally, I bought a gym membership. One day at the gym I was about to give up and one of the trainers there came up and told me that I would never get results working out "like that". I was furious. I was at the gym every morning. He told me that just coming to the gym wouldn't get me in shape. He said walking on the treadmill while reading a magazine, working with the five-pound dumbbells that were easy for me to lift and drinking a protein shake at the end would never accomplish my goals. That's when he said it. "If you really want to change your body, what you do matters less than how you do it."

As mad as I initially was, I spent a couple of days thinking about his statement. After a while, I began to understand his intention and what he meant. I didn't quit the gym and I bought a few training sessions with the guy. It took him three weeks to show me how to properly and more effectively use the same equipment that I had been using for months. My body changed more in two months than it had in five years.

Mrs. Schmidt's story has more than a grain of truth. In fact, each of the methods of Performance-Based Coaching™ described in this chapter can be implemented effectively or they can fail to yield lasting changes in teacher behavior. Both the success and failure of these methods rests not in a coach using the method but using the methods effectively. For each method, the purpose and the steps are listed, along with an analysis of *why* the steps are ordered as they are. Coaches with experience in other models of classroom coaching may find some similarities with what they have done in the past. But what distinguishes Performance-Based Coaching™ from other approaches is both its theoretical foundation and its utilization of very specific methods designed to accelerate human change.

So, let's look at these methods, who they best support and the steps that make each one effective. You will recall from a previous chapter that the coach is required to productively intervene in the learning process of the teacher. We will order the following methods from those that require minimal intervention to those that usually require substantial intervention.

Method #1: Structured Lesson Demonstration
A Valuable First Step, Not a Long-Term Solution

If given the choice of what teachers want coaches to do, without a doubt it would be to conduct in their classrooms one, a few, or a hundred demonstration lessons. Teachers often have an assumption that if they could just "see" what a lesson is supposed to look like with their own students they would then be able to replicate what they observed. This assumption is common in education and reduces effective teaching to a simple exercise in replication of someone else's behavior. By similar logic, one could tune in to two or three episodes of your favorite home remodeling show and then be able to demolish and rebuild your house in a few short weeks.

While watching an activity can be interesting and even informative, to do so with no clear objectives or knowledge to inform the viewing makes it just that – watching something done by someone else. Such a one-way process puts the observer in a very passive role, while the demonstrator assumes responsibility for the totality of the success or failure of the activity. Lesson observations and demonstrations are like Homer's sirens; their gentle calls to come ashore frequently result in nasty crashes against the rocks. Watching another's performance rarely equates to us being able to replicate the performance. When we can't, frustration, blame and bruised ego usually ensue.

Performance-Based Coaching™ utilizes a method known as *Structured Lesson Demonstration* to take advantage of the beneficial aspects of watching an activity while simultaneously keeping the focus on the learner's needs, in this case the teacher. A *Structured Lesson Demonstration* can play a vital role in the coaching process, but not in the way most teachers — or even coaches — anticipate. When trying to accelerate a behavioral change, a *Structured Lesson Demonstration* provides two important outcomes that together form the foundation of the entire coaching partnership. First, a *Structured Lesson Demonstration* provides an opportunity to either challenge or reinforce a teacher's current set of assumptions and beliefs about what their students are capable of doing or learning. Second, a *Structured Lesson Demonstration* builds the coach's credibility as an expert, which in-turn fosters a stronger working relationship between the coach and the teacher. Beyond these initial outcomes, however, additional demonstrations will rarely improve a teacher's mastery of targeted behaviors. Indeed, additional lesson demonstrations can even begin to degrade the repute of the coach as teachers may begin to criticize the actual lesson, or "self-certify" their competence at the behavior due to having "observed" something multiple times.

Coaching Method Steps

1. The coach plans a lesson that explicitly and consistently demonstrates the targeted coaching behavior throughout the entire *Structured Lesson Demonstration*.

2. Before the structured demonstration begins, the coach explains how the target behavior will be demonstrated and how it will advance student learning.

3. The coach conducts the demonstration lesson, which frequently includes comments in real time to the observing teacher about what is happening and why.

4. At the end of the lesson, the coach verbally reiterates how the targeted behavior was implemented.

5. The coach leaves a visual representation or reminder of the targeted coaching behavior in the classroom where it can be easily seen.

A Closer Look At Step 3:

The coach conducts the demonstration lesson, which frequently includes comments in real time to the observing teacher about what is happening and why.

- During your *Structured Lesson Demonstration,* remember that as the coach, you are in control of where the teacher should focus. If they knew exactly what to look for, they wouldn't require this coaching method.

- As you demonstrate each instance of the targeted coaching behavior, articulate to the teacher directly with a **what + why** statement to focus their noticing.

  For example: *Notice that requiring students to verbally use complete sentences at all times (*the what*) gives them practice with academic language structures that they need for writing grade-appropriate academic essays (*the why*).*

By using the structure above, we cue teachers to make the connection between the new behavior and how it impacts student learning, which after all is the rationale for teacher improvement in the first place. You can see that the coach is juggling several balls simultaneously with this coaching method; clearly demonstrating the behavior, cuing the teacher, and helping the teacher to correctly interpret the audible and visual evidence. A *Structured Lesson Demonstration* is quite different than just teaching a lesson while someone watches. The comparison in the box below presents an actual transcription of a traditional demonstration lesson, and then shows the distinctly different role of the coach in a *Structured Lesson Demonstration.*

Traditional Demonstration Lesson	Structured Lesson Demonstration
(The teacher is responsible to observe the coach's behavior without support.)	(The coach shares the responsibility of observation by utilizing *what* + *how* + *why* statements.)
Coach: How might we find the length of the missing side of this shape? **Perimeter = 20** 7 L	Coach: How might we find length of the missing side of this shape? **Perimeter = 20** 7 L
Student[1]: Seven plus something is 20 so we could subtract. 20 − 7 is 13.	Student[1]: Seven plus something is 20 so we could subtract. 20 − 7 is 13.
	Coach to Teacher: I know table three got the answer to this one correct, so I'll have them explain the solution by talking us through the steps, not just telling us the answer.
Coach: You are on the right track with subtracting the side from the perimeter, but I think we might be missing something important. What would we need to find before we subtract?	Coach to Student[1]: You are on the right track with subtracting the side from the perimeter, but I think we might be missing something important. What would we need to find before we subtract?
Student[2]: Two sides are equal to seven and two sides are equal to "L", so we need to subtract 14 from 20 and then split the answer in half to find the missing side.	Student[2]: Two sides are equal to seven and two sides are equal to "L", so we need to subtract 14 from 20 and then split the answer in half to find the missing side.
Coach: So, what would I write down?	Coach: So, what would I write down?
*Continued on the next page	

Continued Traditional Demonstration Lesson	Continued Structured Lesson Demonstration
(The teacher is responsible to observe the coach's behavior without support.)	(The coach shares the responsibility of observation by utilizing *what* + *how* + *why* statements.)
Student[2]: $20-(7 \times 2) = L \times 2$ $\qquad 6 = L \times 2$ $\qquad 3 = L$	Student[2]: $20-(7 \times 2) = L \times 2$ $\qquad 6 = L \times 2$ $\qquad 3 = L$
	Coach to Teacher: Since I want to see if he understands, not just to see if he was listening, I'll have him paraphrase by using a similar problem that requires the same process.
Coach: Perfect. How would we solve this one?	Coach to Student[1]: Perfect. How would we solve this one?
Perimeter = 26	**Perimeter = 26**
L **9**	**L** **9**
Student[1]: We would multiply nine and two, subtract it from the perimeter and divide what's left by two. That gives us 4. L = 4	Student[1]: We would multiply nine and two, subtract it from the perimeter and divide what's left by two. That gives us 4. L = 4
Coach: You got it!	Coach: You got it!

Though there are similarities between both these scenarios, the results are drastically different. In the first scenario, the teacher is left with the entire responsibility for noticing the target behavior, comparing it to their current practice, identifying how and why this version of the behavior is both different and more effective, and doing all of this before figuring out how to best incorporate the new behavior in their own instruction. What's more problematic in the first scenario is that there is no way to be sure if the teacher is actively focusing on the coach or if their attention has shifted to something else: a squirmy student, a pretty handwriting style, voice inflection or any number of other possible distractors. Coaches who have extensive experience demonstrating lessons like the first scenario report that when debriefing with teachers, the teacher often reports having missed the behavior that is the target of the demonstration.

In the second scenario, the coach assumes a greater portion of the responsibility. The coach is now responsible for overtly pointing out the targeted behavior, the rationale for its use and exactly how it should be implemented in the future. This allows the teacher to focus all of their attention on the objective of the demonstration, thus accelerating their learning and providing richer data for the debriefing conversation. This process also accelerates the improvement process as teachers are able to effectively replicate the thought process behind the behavior in an if/then format *If I do this then students will do this.: If this happens then I do this.*

As mentioned earlier, given a choice, teachers typically select lesson observations as their preferred way of working with a coach. Many coaches working within traditional, eclectic, or agnostic coaching paradigms go along with this and conduct lesson demo after lesson demo for their teachers. Not surprisingly, teachers are happy because they typically do not relish the idea of conducting a lesson independently in front of their coach. Their happiness and comfort though, come at the cost of behavioral change for the benefit of students. One-way observations in some organizations are sometimes equated by teachers as part of the formalized teacher evaluation system employed in most schools and districts.

Performance-Based Coaching™, and its related methods, regularly involves teachers and coaches together in classrooms where either one or both of the parties are teaching. Because we view coaching always as a collaborative endeavor, coach and teacher frequently have opportunities to see the other "in action." This type of observation is viewed as a natural and important part of coaching, since by observing one another and by collaboratively teaching, each can better gather and analyze information that directly informs both the process of coaching and the end product.

Coaching Tip

It is always more effective to plan one to two ways that the targeted behavior can be implemented during a *Structured Lesson Demonstration* and repeat them consistently than it is to plan a multitude of examples. Remember, we want more people doing fewer things better, so help your teachers to not have to hunt for your great examples.

As you determine which teachers can benefit from the use of this method, it can be helpful to keep three teacher characteristics in mind.

Who Benefits Most from *Structured Lesson Demonstrations*?		
Teacher Experience	Overall Skill Level	Level of Independence
Best suited for teachers with greater levels of experience as it challenges assumptions related to what is possible for their students.	Best suited for teachers with greater levels of skill as they may be able to implement observed practices with less explanation.	*Structured Lesson Demonstrations* do not support the development of teacher independence and should therefore be used strategically.
Less suited for teachers with little to no experience as there is a greater chance of overgeneralizing.	Less suited for teachers with lower skill levels as they may struggle to implement a practice they have observed without detailed explanation.	

Coaching Method #2: Data-Driven Observation
A Collection of Change Evidence Over Time

Used most often at the beginning of a coaching cycle, a *Data-Driven Observation* provides a quantitative record of the starting point for the collaborative work. This data is then shared and used by the coach and teacher to set goals for the coaching cycle and to determine which coaching methods should be used to bring about the desired change. It is important to emphasize that *Data-Driven Observations* are not conducted in isolation; they simply serve as the best way to describe something at the beginning of a process, and then again at the end. They provide a snapshot of a teacher's use and mastery of a given behavior or set of behaviors at a certain time. Because this type of observation collects only visual or auditory evidence of the behavior, it provides teachers with a source of factual and objective evidence. Thus, instead of a teacher hearing something like, "You're doing much better now with student questioning than when we started," as they would hear from a traditional style coach, they hear something far more powerful and affirming of the important work they have done.

> *"You see from the data that 92% of your questions of students are being responded to in complete sentences. Remember when we started that the percentage was less than 20."*

Coaching Method Steps

1.   The coach clearly defines what observable behavior is being measured. All relevant terms are defined.

2.   The coach enters the room and sits in a single location, minimizing impact on the lesson.

3. The coach transcribes or collects quantitative data related to the defined behavior.

4. The coach analyzes the data and shares conclusions regarding the behavior with the teacher.

5. The coach sets a goal for the coaching cycle.

Coaching Tip

Remember, the only behaviors that can be controlled in the classroom are the behaviors of the teacher. We only observe the teacher during a *Data-Driven Observation* as it minimizes the variables and focuses the change process where it is most important — on the teacher.

A Closer Look At Step 3

The coach transcribes or collects quantitative data related to the defined behavior.

Data-Driven Observation is for observing and recording data based on a quantitative question. This focus on the quantitative removes the perceived subjectivity of a qualitative data collection and further separates the process from that of evaluation. These observations are meant to be brief, usually not longer than 10 minutes in length.

Note: As *Structured Lesson Demonstration* and *Data-Driven Observation* place greater responsibility on only one side of the coaching partnership, they tend to have less overall impact on behavioral change than other methods to follow that feature more intervention by the coach. Think of *Data-Driven Observation* like checking your blood pressure. The act of checking it repeatedly will not fix the problem. Checking your blood pressure at given intervals as new diets and exercise programs are implemented can, however, ensure that progress is being made or indicate that alternative interventions are needed.

- When collecting data, make sure you are asking a quantitative question.

- *Data-Driven Observation* answers questions like: How many...? How often...? or What percentage ...? These questions frequently tackle total quantity with respect to time and opportunity. The table below shows you the difference between qualitative questions that beget meaningless generalizations versus quantitative questions that collect specific, mathematical evidence that charts performance at the beginning, middle and end of a coaching cycle.

Qualitative Classroom Observation Question	Quantitative Data-Driven Observation Question.
1. Is the lesson aligned to an objective?	How many questions does the teacher ask that directly relate to the posted objective?
	How often is a question posed to the class that is directly related to the posted objective?
	What percentage of the questions asked are directly related to the posted objective?
2. Is the lesson rigorous?	How many *why* or *how* questions were asked during the lesson?
	How often were students asked to expand or elaborate upon an initial response?
	What percentage of student responses were directly followed by another question instead of a statement made by the teacher?

The types of questions above bring about certain types of data. Again, the qualitative questions bring about answers that defy clear action or specificity and are interpretations of evidence. The quantitative questions, by contrast, yield clear and objective collections of actionable data. Here is another comparison of the two approaches.

Is the lesson aligned to an objective?

Qualitative Classroom Observation Data	Quantitative Data-Driven Observation Data
Though the objectives were posted at the front of the room, the lesson was not focused or aligned to what was posted.	From 10:00a.m. – 10:15a.m. you asked three questions that directly related to the posted objective. Students were asked one question that related to the posted objective every five minutes. Of the 10 questions that were asked, 30% of them related to the posted objective.

Is the lesson rigorous?

Qualitative Classroom Observation Data	Quantitative Data-Driven Observation Data
Some students were not challenged during the lesson. The questions were low-level recall-based questions that didn't require much analysis or application.	From 11:15a.m. – 11:30a.m. students were asked one "why" (rationale) question and they were never asked a "how do you know" (justification) question. Two students were asked to add to their initially formulated responses. Of the 15 student responses observed, follow-up questions were posed 13% of the time, while teacher explanation was provided 65% of the time and a new line of questioning was initiated 22% of the time after an initial student response.

These two approaches offer fundamentally different information to teachers. The feedback conclusions on the left side are vague and provide little in the way of benchmarking performance or providing evidence of mastery or improvement. Qualitative questions also work against multiple observers using the same data set with which to draw conclusions or to formulate plans, since each observer (read: interpreter) sees what he or she sees in their own idiosyncratic way. As mentioned previously, qualitative data begets interpretation, which begets uncertainly, defensiveness and opinion.

By focusing on quantitative questions and their corresponding data, teachers are given a benchmark of their current performance. Future data points provide a clear indicator of whether the target behavior is more frequent or less frequent. This also provides teachers a way to self-monitor their own performance indicators and continue to focus on coaching goals outside of regular coaching sessions. Some coaching approaches that rely on qualitative data collection further complicate matters. Instead of presenting a factual evidence record for the teacher to analyze, the coach proceeds with a cognitive or affective line of questioning that usually further muddies the water.

Cognitive

If you were to do this lesson again, what might you change?

If you knew students were only going to respond to your questions with one word, what other strategy could you have implemented to get a complete sentence?

Would your approach have been different if all of these students were native English speakers?

Affective

How did you feel that the lesson went?

Do you feel that students gained new knowledge from this lesson?

How did you feel when students were unable to answer the final question?

The logical end point for the post-lesson, cognitive game of hypothesizing is that teachers are left to either defend their previous actions or to answer the question, thus tacitly acknowledging that their approach was flawed. At some point, teachers who are put through this game of Groundhog Day are left with no clear conclusions or plans. At its most illogical, teachers wonder why the coach wouldn't have provided better solutions if their performance was inadequate. After all, wouldn't they have done something differently or better if they had known how?

The use of affective questions invites a strange feelings-fest whereby the learning outcomes for students are far less important than how the teacher felt about the lesson. Facts have no feelings, but by using affective metrics for determining the lesson's impact, coaches are transformed into therapists who must accept the teacher's feelings as valid and as conclusive of what actually happened.

By relying solely on quantitative data, the conversation moves away from silly hypothetical guessing games and emotion-soaked justifications to a simple statement of logic that is easily understandable, defensible and actionable: "By doing behavior X more frequently, students will be able to do Y better." This shift gives teachers a clear goal. It also points to a behavior that they can both plan into their lesson and self-monitor during instruction.

Remember, *Data-Driven Observation* does not teach a new method or accelerate the development of instructional skills. It is only beneficial as a way to monitor behavioral change in real time and provide evidence of need or evidence of improvement.

Who Benefits the Most from *Data-Driven Observation?*		
Teacher Experience	Overall Skill Level	Independence Level
The use of D*ata-Driven Observation* is not dependent on experience.	The use of D*ata-Driven Observation* is not dependent on skill.	*Data-Driven Observation* does not by itself develop independence but is effective for showing developing independence.

Method #3: *Real-Time Corrective Feedback*
Improving Performance in the Moment

As described in the previous section, teachers are frequently asked by coaches to reflect on a recently completed lesson with questions such as, "If you were to do this lesson again…?" This question, though noble in its cause to foster reflection, is incredibly flawed due to the nature of real classroom instruction. Teachers make sometimes hundreds of decisions in real-time during every lesson. To ask or to tell teachers how they could, would, or should respond differently in the future places their lesson and all its variables in a vacuum that is unlikely to ever occur together that way again. For these reasons, coaching must happen *during* the teaching. *Real-Time Corrective Feedback* is a coaching method that is pretty similar to how we conduct our real lives. When two friends are sharing a Mexican food lunch, they are likely to share their enjoyment, or lack thereof, of the food and then inquire about the same of their companion. Whether the food is good or bad, it is during the meal that such a discussion is held. It's not likely that three weeks after the lunch, one of the friends would call the other to inquire as to their comments about the Mexican food lunch they shared the prior month. In short, feedback is maximally valuable during the game, in the heat of the action, while the event is ongoing, and everyone sees the same things and has the same information.

Different from our first two methods where the coach was "outside the action" and physically on the periphery of the room, in *Real-Time Corrective Feedback* the coach physically positions him or herself near the teacher so as to be able to lean in and speak to the teacher during the lesson. The coach will sit to the side of the lesson until it is necessary to provide real-time feedback, which is provided in close proximity to the teacher, but it is not treated as a top-level secret that demands whispering or a cone of silence. In this method, coaches put down their notepads and actively observe the lesson for opportunities to provide directives, reminders, quick definitions or other useful information to the teacher related to the coaching goal. When the coach observes a strategic opportunity to intervene, the coach stands and approaches the teacher in order to provide a brief, succinct, and do-able prompt or directive that the teacher implements immediately. The coach then retracts himself or herself from the lesson until the next opportunity for either refinement or enhancement arises. This method allows a coach and a teacher to work together in real-time to improve instruction in a way that eliminates hindsight and explicitly focuses on the targeted behavior within the authentic context of teaching and learning.

Coaching Method Steps

1. The coach positions himself or herself in the room near where the teacher is standing or sitting.

2. The coach attentively observes for opportunities where the targeted coaching behavior should have been implemented or could be better implemented.

3. The coach steps into the lesson.

4. The coach provides a clear coaching prompt or directive.

5. The coach steps out of the lesson and continues attentively observing for opportunities to assist the teacher to implement the targeted coaching behavior successfully.

Coaching Tip

Think like a football coach. It can feel impossible to communicate with your players during game action, so it's OK to call a timeout. Watch for times that are natural breaks in the lesson to step-in, i.e., during partner talk, think time, when students are writing, etc.

A Closer Look At Step 4
The Coaching Command – Clear and Actionable

- When stepping into the lesson, the goal is to quickly, clearly and succinctly provide a directive or prompt to the teacher that triggers or calls for the use of the targeted behavior.

- Always begin your coaching intervention with an action-oriented verb. It is the observable action that you want the teacher to do immediately after you step out of the lesson. This will minimize the interaction time and keep the flow of the lesson intact. The teacher should not have to guess as to what you are asking him or her to do or say.

The short scenario below sets the stage for better understanding this critical coach behavior. The first graphic gives several examples of poor and ineffective feedback. In the right column is an explanation for why such comments are not useful. Further on, examples of effective verbal interventions are provided, along with a rationale for their utility.

In a fifth-grade classroom, students discuss a question posed to the class with their groups. One group finishes their discussion. A second group sits quietly waiting for someone to begin the conversation. The rest of the groups are actively talking about the prompt. The teacher walks around and asks students to restate what they have discussed to ensure that each group is staying on topic.

As the teacher walks back to the front of the room, the coach steps in and says:

Ineffective Coaching Feedback (Though real-time in nature, this type of feedback leaves the teacher unsure of how exactly to proceed.)	Why This Type of Feedback Does Not Help?
"How could you get the group that has finished talking to discuss the topic at a deeper level?"	Asking the teacher a question during their lesson is an invitation to dialogue that can stall the lesson and does not provide a clear picture of what to do next? Discussions like these are more useful for co-planning or training sessions but are frustrating to the teacher and ineffective at changing behavior during real-time coaching.

Ineffective Coaching Feedback (Though real-time in nature, this type of feedback leaves the teacher unsure of how exactly to proceed.)	Why This Type of Feedback Does Not Help?
The group over there is just sitting quietly. You should go over and help them get started.	By starting with the rationale and not the action verb, the teacher immediately focuses on the initial statement. This distracts from the change in behavior that should be the focus of the coaching interaction. Also, the verb "help" does not connote a clear observable behavior. What does *help* look like? Comments like these will often be immediately followed by the teacher asking "How?"
I love how you are walking around and monitoring for engagement. Now that the students are mostly engaged, let's try to up the rigor of the lesson so that the students can use higher levels of cognition. Maybe you could differentiate the question between those two groups since one group is done and the other hasn't really started yet.	Though it feels good to initiate interactions with a positive statement or a compliment, this feedback moves the focus away from what exactly the teacher needs to do next. The length of this statement also changes this interaction from a strategic coaching intervention to a mini discussion or lecture, leaving the teacher feeling like they are back in a college classroom.

These coaching interactions represent three common mistakes coaches make when first starting to implement *Real-Time Corrective Feedback*. Yes, all three are examples of feedback, and yes, all three are in real time. But none of these are examples of how to effectively implement this method. Let's look at how the coaching commands should have been stated using the same scenario.

In the same fifth-grade classroom, students discuss a question posed to the class with their groups. One group finishes their discussion. A second group sits quietly waiting for someone to begin the conversation. The rest of the groups are actively talking about the prompt. The teacher walks around and asks students to restate what they have discussed to ensure that each group is staying on topic.

As the teacher walks back to the front of the room, the coach steps in and says:

Verb-Driven Coaching Interventions (These are direct statements that leave the teacher understanding exactly how to proceed with their instruction.)	Why This Type of Feedback Helps?
(Pointing to the finished group) -Tell that group how you would answer the question. Then ask them, "How was their answer different than yours?" That will give them a *Push!* to go beyond what they actually did.	Verbs like "tell" and "ask" leave no room for interpretation. The teacher knows exactly what you want them to do next and can implement the coaching command quickly.
(Pointing to the group that hasn't begun) – Ask that group to choose between two possible answers. Then, tell them to discuss why that was their choice since they haven't said anything yet.	By moving the rationale to the end of the coaching command, the teacher can keep their focus on what to do next (the behavior) while still being given the information regarding why the change is being made.
Stop the class. Change the question to, "(Say the exact question you want the teacher to use.)" Then send them back to their discussion.	In some cases, providing a clear coaching command means providing the teacher with the exact words that you want them to use. Remember, if they knew exactly what question they should have asked, or what statement they should have said, wouldn't they have done that in the first place?

When it comes to *Real-Time Corrective Feedback,* the verbal coaching directives that we choose as coaches are as vital as the timeliness and brevity of the interaction. When done correctly, coaching interactions rarely exceed three-to-five seconds and teachers (and frequently students) can see the benefit of the coaching interaction immediately.

Who Benefits the Most from *Real-Time Corrective Feedback?*		
Teacher Experience	Overall Skill Level	Level of Independence
The use of *Real-Time Corrective Feedback* is equally effective across all levels of experience.	Teachers with greater levels of skill require commands that clearly define what to do next, while struggling teachers often require commands that define both what to say and do next.	*Real-Time Corrective Feedback* is highly effective at building independence, as the coach can easily control the amount and frequency of support.

Things To Ponder Or Discuss

1. Why is it important to remember that "methods" are step-by-step processes that are designed to bring about a specific outcome? What are some of the risks of using methods that have no clear steps?

2. Is it fair to say that most teachers would prefer a traditional "lesson demo" over having to do a lesson with other adults present?

3. Is the fear that coaching is a surreptitious way of evaluating teachers a realistic concern in your current or likely coaching situation?

4. Why is the idea of working with teachers in real time so provocative? Can you think of other professions where feedback is provided well after the completion of an activity or task?

5. Should coaches coach other coaches on their actual coaching practices in real time also?

6. Who on your staff could you imagine immediately seeing the benefits of real-time coaching? Can you think of someone who would be against it? What do you make of their arguments in favor or against it?

The Coaches Corner

In a previous chapter you listened in on two coaches (Jennifer and Rosalina) discussing their experiences as coaches from two distinctly different paradigms. It is likely that you will, sooner or later, have to explain to your teachers the differences between coaching as they probably know it, or imagine it, and Performance-Based Coaching™. Use the organizer below to identify at least four differences between coaching models that your teachers will need to understand.

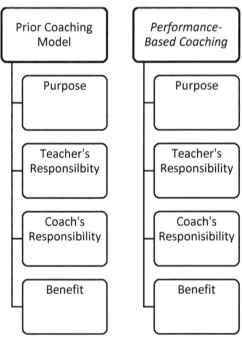

Now, using the information in the column on the right, write a paragraph, suitable for publication, that clearly and convincingly supports the use of the theory, principles and methods of Performance-Based Coaching™ at your school or in your district. This may prove to be one of your most important written products.

Tip: Don't assume that anyone on your staff fully understands or understood the prior or current approach to coaching. Don't assume that they understand Performance-Based Coaching™ any better. Time invested now will be well spent.

The Leaders Lounge

Rightly or wrongly, many of the teachers on your staff are likely to believe that coaching programs are really covert administrative evaluation schemes. If you as leader of your organization fail to neutralize this sentiment, it will be your coach or coaches who will have to take responsibility for addressing this – and that is clearly not a proper role or function for any coach.

Here is how you can address this real or potential situation. Answer the following questions in writing. By combining your answers, you will have a ready-made response to any aspersions cast on your coaching program.

1. What is the historical context of coaching at your site and in your district? When did it happen, if ever? Why did it happen? What happened to it? Who sponsored it? How was it paid for? What were the outcomes?

2. What about the historical context above may have led people to believe coaching was actually used for teacher evaluation purposes or for other nefarious reasons? List the reasons for

such beliefs, and then assign them a veracity rating from 1-10, with a score of 10 meaning that it is true and actually did happen. A score of 1 or 2 means that, from your analysis, you have deduced it is nothing more than an urban myth.

3. What is the purpose of implementing Performance-Based Coaching™ now? The purpose can be determined by filling in the blank in the statement, "We are doing this now because _____."

4. What are five benefits that you, as captain of the ship, see ahead if coaching is implemented as detailed in this book? Benefits are a way of painting an image of what could happen in the future. For this exercise, confine all of your benefits to those that would accrue to the adults who work in your school or district. Motivations to participate are always personal, so help your people out with this by telling them of the benefits.

Tip: Remember Alice, Biff and Carla and what each of them is listening for.

Put these all together and you are prepared to address most of the most pervasive –and usually unfounded — negative aspersions about coaching. More important, you are shifting the dialogue away from disabling conspiracy theories to the bright sunshine of possibility.

Fun Quiz

1. In my opinion, most people love being coached in most all of their activities.

           Agree   Disagree   Not Sure

2. The provision of real-time feedback means that feedback is happening _____ instruction.

   a. after
   b. before
   c. during
   d. alongside

3. Traditional lesson demonstrations serve mainly to take the focus away from _____ performance and redirect it on _____ performance.

   a. teaching, teachers
   b. teacher, coach
   c. coach, teacher
   d. instruction, learning

4. In Performance-Based Coaching™, a coach has to simultaneously focus on the teacher's _____ and the teacher's _____.

   a. lesson, engagement
   b. lesson, behaviors
   c. behaviors, aptitude
   d. performance, independence

5. A big part of coaching is to help teachers to _____.

   a. observe
   b. record data
   c. engage
   d. notice

Chapter 8
The Methods Of Performance-Based Coaching
Part Two

Introduction

In this chapter we will continue learning about the methods of Performance-Based Coaching™. You will see as you read through these methods that the role of the coach takes on some expanded functions compared to the first three methods covered in the previous chapter. Much like coaches help teachers to improve their performance, the behaviors required of coaches require careful study, preparation and practice. It is important to emphasize that, although we are presenting these methods in groups to highlight their commonalities, they should not be viewed as linear; we don't necessarily start with method number 1 and continue through methods 2-8. Instead, much like a physician diagnoses and then prescribes, the skillful Performance-Based Coach™ analyzes a teacher's current level of competence with a particular behavior, sets the plan and begins its execution.

Objectives

In this chapter you will learn:

1. How the role and functions of a coach can take different forms during a lesson depending on the coaching method employed;

2. The high level of responsibility borne by Performance-Based Coaches™ to ensure that each minute of a lesson is valuable for the teacher and is not lost instructional time for students;

3. How the coach's use of language during a coaching session sets the tone for a positive work session that is characterized by accurate and productive exchanges that enhance behavioral change;

4. Three methods of Performance-Based Coaching™ and their applications.

You Have Probably Seen Or Heard This Before

An interesting aspect of most people is that we all can get bored sometimes of a similar routine, activity or even of a familiar face or group of people. We deal with that boredom or fatigue by managing the amount of time we do something or see someone, or by decreasing the frequency of an activity or interaction. Even with a much-loved hobby or friend, we sometimes need time alone to recharge. We then come back with renewed energy. Much the same thing can and does happen with coaching. But we have learned over two decades that much of the boredom and lack of progress expressed by both coaches and teachers related to coaching has to do with the paucity — or total absence — of actual coaching methods.   Listen to Marcy, a kindergarten teacher, talk about how a desire to be coached turned sour.

> *I was gung ho for the coaching program at my school. I think a lot of us were. But once we got coached three or four times, it seemed like it lacked direction and was the same exact thing over and over again. Our coach – who we all liked as a person – would just show up, observe our lesson, and then talk to us afterward about what happened. Whether we were a first-year teacher or a 20-year veteran, we all got the same thing. And we got it over and over again until it just became played out.*

While adding variety just to have variety is probably not the answer, you can see that the progression of the methods of Performance-Based Coaching™ is both responsive to a certain teacher need while also offering a level of newness and purpose that serves to keep the coaching process energized. Let's be honest: coaches too need some variety in their day to stay focused and motivated to do the sometimes-heavy lifting related to that important role. We will continue our methods exploration with one that transforms both the role of the teacher and the coach and opens a door to some dynamic within-lesson feedback and dialogue.

Method #4: *Pass the Pen*
Like An Acrobat, Some Teachers Need To Work With A Safety Net

Teaching can be a highly personal profession. Many teachers internalize every aspect of their classroom to the point that any suggestion for change can be stressful and intimidating. In order to help these teachers to try new methods, Performance-Based Coaches™ provide the safety net that supports them should they begin to lose their balance or fall. In *Pass the Pen*, the coach positions himself or herself in the same way that they would for *Real-time Corrective Feedback*, that is, within three or four feet of the teacher. The control point of this method is a shared marker, or piece of chalk, that the coach and teacher take turns using to teach the lesson. Typically, the teacher initiates the lesson and continues until they identify a point in the instruction where they would like to "pass the pen" in order to observe and learn more about a particular behavior. At that point, the coach assumes the pen for as long as necessary to perform the target behavior, usually with a short comment or point of feedback that is designed to help the teacher. The coach then passes the pen back to the teacher.

The flow of the lesson is not disturbed because the teacher and coach trade positions quickly. Even though the teacher may pass control to the coach as often as they wish, the coach can manage the process by short interventions followed by a return of the pen to the teacher. This exchange of the pen — analogous to the baton in relay racing — provides the teacher with a safe way out of a sticky spot or a way to signal a request for assistance during a lesson at the exact moment a new behavior or skill is needed. *Pass the Pen* also has proven to help teachers to better anticipate opportunities to use a new skill or behavior as they learn to structure lessons in ways that are more productive for students.

Coaching Method Steps

1. Before the lesson, the coach and the teacher predetermine the object to be traded (pen, chalk) and a signal to trade positions.

2. The coach positions himself or herself in close proximity to the teacher.

3. The coach observes the lesson for the targeted teacher behavior.

4. The coach or the teacher signals — and passes the pen — when an opportunity for the targeted behavior occurs.

5. The coach and the teacher trade places. The coach demonstrates the targeted behavior.

6. The coach and the teacher trade places again and the teacher repeats the behavior as it was demonstrated.

7. This sequence is repeated throughout the lesson as determined by coach and teacher.

Coaching Tip

Pass the Pen is a method that keeps coaches on their toes, since you never know when a teacher may signal for support. This is also a method that can be used to build confidence and independence when the coach withholds the trading of places. If you have observed the teacher correctly implementing the targeted behavior previously, increase the sophistication of the targeted behavior by using a coaching command or short demonstration that is beyond the teacher's current level of skillful implementation.

A Closer Look at Step 3
Wait For My Signal – The Art Of The Switch

*   Like *Real Time Corrective Feedback*, *Pass the Pen* is one of the most utilized methods in a Performance-Based Coaching™ program. This method can either be the focus of an entire coaching session or used during the implementation of any

of the other coaching methods to enhance their effectiveness.

- This method is frequently the answer when you have worked with a teacher who, for whatever reasons, is resisting a new behavior or failing to consistently implement it. *Pass the Pen* takes advantage of an actual lesson to repeatedly place the teacher in situations where the targeted behavior would be helpful to students' learning. You will see below a very sophisticated way of getting a teacher to utilize a behavior they have resisted.

Let's look at three instances when *Pass the Pen* should be used to accelerate a desired change in teacher behavior.

Utilization	Navigating the Switch
Pass the Pen – As the prescribed coaching method	You see an alternative way to implement an aspect of the lesson, but it requires more than a single coaching command.
	At a natural break in instruction — while students are talking, as a teacher writes something on the board, or at the end of a sentence during a lecture — signal the teacher to switch places.
	Demonstrate the practice that you want the teacher to implement. Before signaling the teacher to trade places again, overtly tell the students what the teacher is going to do when they re-enter the lesson. Ex: "OK! Now, Mr. Clark is going to ask you to _____."

Utilization	Navigating the Switch
Pass the Pen – To bring a teacher into a *Structured Lesson Demonstration*	You are demonstrating for a teacher that has a functional level of skill but lacks confidence in their ability to implement a new practice. Schedule the lesson as a *Structured Lesson Demonstration*. Choose a targeted behavior that you want the teacher to practice implementing. During the demonstration, when the targeted behavior is appropriate, approach the teacher. Tell them what you are about to do. Tell them that you will signal to them and they will then do the same thing. Then the coach will continue with the lesson.
Pass the Pen – To clarify a *Real-Time Corrective Feedback* coaching command	You step in to provide a clear coaching command. As you begin to step back out of the lesson, the teacher pauses or looks at you with confusion. Immediately, signal to the teacher to switch places and step back into the lesson. Demonstrate exactly the coaching command you provided and signal the teacher to switch back into the lesson. At the next appropriate opportunity, use the same clear coaching command that you demonstrated during the last switch.

Pass the Pen is a powerful coaching method, but it can quickly become addictive to some teachers, as they know you are willing to step in and take control of the lesson at a moment's notice. Remember that, as the coach, you are in control of the coaching methods and their proper utilization. You are also responsible for ensuring that the coaching time does not sacrifice students' learning time. If a teacher signals that they need to switch places with you too often, or as a way to avoid trying a new practice, it is perfectly acceptable to step in, provide a clear coaching command and allow the teacher to continue the lesson.

Avoid allowing your time in control of the lesson to extend beyond the targeted behavior that you are demonstrating. *Pass the Pen* is best used as a brief demonstration of a targeted behavior that can be immediately replicated by the teacher. It is not the coach's license to highjack the lesson nor is it a teacher's free pass to have the coach conduct the entirety of the lesson.

Who Benefits the Most from *Pass the Pen?*		
Teacher Experience	Overall Skill Level	Level of Independence
The use of *Pass the Pen* is equally effective across all levels of experience.	Because the passing of the pen is controlled by the teacher, it allows teachers of all levels to self-diagnose areas of need or further development. It can be especially helpful for teachers with lower skill levels who benefit from the immediacy and relevance of the coach's mediations and directives.	*Pass the Pen* is highly effective at building independence, as the coach can easily control the amount and frequency of support across a coaching cycle.

Method #5: *Narrated Lesson*
A Mediated Demonstration That Highlights Proper Procedure

One of the first thoughts teachers usually have after learning a new method or being asked to implement a new program is something like, "That looks great, but will it work for me and my students?" Though coaches habitually tackle these apprehensive thoughts through limited repetitions of *Structured Lesson Demonstration*, often the observing teacher is not aware of the nuances that they are witnessing, or the thought processes used by the teacher to make instructional decisions in real time. *Narrated Lesson Demonstration* provides Performance-Based Coaches™ with a structure for verbally analyzing with the coachee a lesson conducted by a teacher well-skilled in the target behavior. Thus, the successful utilization of this method involves three people: the coach, the teacher, and a demonstrating teacher. This coaching method places the coach and the observing teacher out of the way of the lesson so that they can quietly discuss the instruction they are watching. Another major benefit of this coaching method is that it shows teachers two important things. First, it provides evidence that the method or behavior utilized skillfully by the demonstrating teacher is indeed possible and beneficial for students, and second, that other teachers have gained a high level of competence in its use through coaching. This can sometimes remove a false assumption that only coaches can utilize correctly a new method or certain behavior.

Coaching Method Steps

1. The coach selects a teacher who can skillfully demonstrate the targeted behavior for the coach and the teacher.

2. The coach defines the targeted behavior for the observing teacher prior to the lesson.

3. The coach and the observing teacher sit in one location, minimizing impact on the lesson.

4. The coach quietly points out the use of the target behavior throughout the lesson.

5. The coach and the teacher return to the classroom to implement the targeted behavior immediately.

Coaching Tip

Narrated Lesson is a great method for building confidence and independence for the demonstrating teacher. Set him or her up for success by requesting permission to observe the skillful use of a behavior they have learned to use during their own coaching cycles. This demonstration also provides a coach with a window into how effectively the demonstrating teacher continues to utilize a particular behavior. Everyone likes to be recognized, and your demonstrating teacher will undoubtedly be proud that you have involved them in the teacher learning process. And by the way, this is a tangible example of what building system-wide capacity is all about.

A Closer Look At Step 4
Narrating For Others - Report The News and Save The Editorial

- A lesson narration that utilizes the classroom and teaching skills of another educator can be a powerful way to show a teacher what is possible during instruction.

- It is vital that the narration that occurs at the back of the classroom focuses on the frequency of a target behavior or a description of the target behavior as it occurs.

- Avoid comments about the quality of instruction. Evaluative or interpretive commentary does little to change teacher behavior and can harm the relationship between teachers and the coach.

- Think of lesson narration as analogous to filling out a disciplinary referral or a police report. Ensure all comments are objective and observable.

Let's take a look at two possible scenarios for lesson narration and how they might affect the change process. In the left column are comments that report "just the news", consistent with the steps of this method. On the right you will see examples of subjectivity and interpretation, which almost always result in less-than-favorable acceptance by most people.

Objective Lesson Narration (Focus on quantitative and descriptive narrations.)	**Subjective Lesson Narration** (Focus on subjective or evaluative narrations.)
Coach: During the lesson we will count the number of times that Mrs. Hanson elicits complete sentence answers from her students.	Coach: Mrs. Hanson is really good at getting students to produce oral language. We are going to watch for how she does it.
(Coach and teacher enter the room)	(Coach and teacher enter the room)
Coach: She is eliciting a repeated response in the form of a complete sentence.	Coach: We don't always want to get students to repeat things, but it is OK at the beginning of the lesson.
Coach: Now, she is offering them a choice of options, both of which are in complete sentence form.	See how she offered that group a choice when they didn't know the answer? That is a really good way to get students talking.
Coach: Watch how she asks the students what question they would ask next before providing her own question.	Shelly is one of the best at getting the students to ask questions. This is what you need to do more of next week. Ask them what questions they would ask, then have them answer each other.
This is the fourth opportunity for students to talk or write in complete sentences during the past 10 minutes.	See how often she is getting students to talk. Let's focus on getting students to talk this often during your lessons. That will really help.

These two approaches offer fundamentally different information to the teacher who is observing an expert with the goal of mastering a specific behavior. The version on the left is an objective and descriptive exercise that facilitates future coaching sessions. The version from the right column is an interpretive and evaluative exercise that compares the skill level of a teacher to their peers and does little to facilitate future change. The terms are so loosely defined as to be meaningless.

Who Benefits the Most from *Narrated Lesson?*		
Teacher Experience	Overall Skill Level	Level of Independence
Less effective for teachers with greater experience as many teachers have the tendency to begin justifying their practices by observing for similarities.	This method can be enlightening for teachers of all skill levels. It provides all teachers with a new way to observe and discuss instruction using quantitative terms.	*Narrated Lesson* can be highly effective to support the development of independence for the demonstrating teacher.
Highly effective for teachers with less experience as it can offer additional ways that a targeted behavior can be implemented.	Less effective for teachers with lower levels of skill as it removes them from the context of their own classroom.	*Narrated Lesson* does not directly support the development of independence for the observing teacher.

Method #6: *Co-Plan/Co-Teach*
A True Partnership For Growth

Up to now, our methods have involved the Performance-Based Coach™ working in real time with teachers and their students. The next method, called *Co-Plan/ Co-Teach*, groups the coach and teacher together to plan and deliver a lesson that incorporates the focus areas of their work up to that time. Such before-lesson collaboration allows for a rich flow of dialogue as both educators actively craft a lesson plan that strategically incorporates certain behaviors and skills. As useful as this planning time is, we must acknowledge that it also requires a substantial time investment, thus its use may be less frequent than other real-time coaching methods. Still, effective *Co-Plan/Co-Teach* sessions can happen in 20-30 minutes; they are not multi-hour curriculum planning meetings that require catered food and multiple television monitors.

The objective of this method is for both coach and teacher to equally share responsibility for the planning, preparation, and delivery of a lesson. Logically, the coach and the teacher meet before the lesson to plan the procedures, assign roles for who will teach which portion of the lesson, and set a desired and measurable coaching objective. The team then teaches the lesson together according to their agreed-upon plan and then meets to discuss the attainment of the coaching objectives after the lesson. This method sets teachers up for maximum success by making sure that quality preparation has occurred before the lesson. It also provides coaches with a rich stream of information and understanding about how a teacher approaches lesson design and delivery.

Coaching Method Steps

1. The coach (and sometimes the coach and the teacher) defines the targeted coaching behavior that will be overtly planned into the lesson.

2. The teacher identifies the content and lesson objective that will be taught.

3. The coach and the teacher separate the lesson into discrete segments and decide who will teach which segment.

4. The coach and the teacher plan how the targeted coaching behavior will be implemented throughout each segment of the lesson.

5. The coach and the teacher deliver the lesson together, each instructing their respective portions of the lesson.

6. The coach and the teacher discuss the use of the target coaching behavior (or behaviors) after the lesson.

7. The coach sets a goal for the continued use of the targeted behavior in subsequent lessons.

Coaching Tip

When choosing which portions of the lesson you and the teacher will each personally instruct, use *Co-Plan/Co-Teach* as an opportunity to push the teacher to work in areas in which the probability of success is high. The coach should teach those segments that allow for showing the teacher how to use the target behavior with greater sophistication. But if the teacher can do it, they should do it.

A Closer Look At Step 2
The Right Questions – A Window Into Teachers' Thinking

• Unfortunately, most opportunities for teachers to collaboratively design and implement lessons occurs only during their college preparation or student teaching experience. As a result, most of their thinking about lesson structure and such happens within their own heads. By working with a teacher before the lesson is delivered, coaches have a unique opportunity to ask questions, ask for elaboration, and explore in greater detail the assumptions and beliefs their teachers have about teaching, learning, personal change and many other relevant topics. This is also an opportune time to ask specific questions about the lesson's content and related concepts to ensure everyone has a good grasp of the subject matter. The examples below show how those types of questions might be phrased.

During the *Co-Plan* portion of the method, utilize the following questions to help you and your teacher to better understand the various elements that go into the lesson. Note the questions that are difficult for the teacher to articulate and focus your planning time on helping them come to a clear response.

It is important to ask the questions in this order, as subsequent questions build on the previously asked questions.

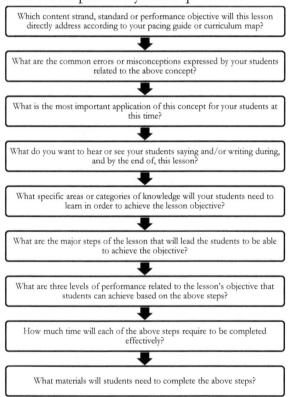

Sometimes it helps to pose two or three of the first questions on this list to the teacher prior to your planning session. This will allow the teacher to come prepared to the co-planning session with clear ideas or questions.

Who Benefits the Most from *Co-Plan/Co-Teach*?		
Teacher Experience	Overall Skill Level	Level of Independence
The use of *Co-Plan/Co-Teach* is equally effective across all levels of experience.	This method is most effective for teachers who have demonstrated that lesson planning could be improved. Even highly skilled teachers can benefit from a coach's input during the lesson-planning process.	The use of *Co-Plan/Co-Teach* can be highly effective to support the development of independence when the responsibility for delivery of certain behaviors and skills is assigned strategically.

Things To Ponder Or Discuss

1. Describe what you believe is a solid rationale for grouping the methods of Performance-Based Coaching™ as they are in this book?

2. Have you ever had an expert coach narrate another teacher's lesson while you both observed it? Why or why not? What did you learn from the experience?

3. What is your explanation of why qualitative language for discussing teachers, teaching, student learning and school performance is so pervasive?

4. Describe what you envision as teachers' reactions to the coaching methods described so far in this book.

5. At this point in your understanding of Performance-Based Coaching™, why do you think some schools and districts adopt one of the other coaching approaches discussed earlier? Why would some choose to proceed with an "eclectic" or "agnostic" model?

The Coaches Corner

Learning to observe, analyze and talk about instruction through a quantitative lens can sometimes be an on-going challenge for coaches. We are far more accustomed in education to using qualitative descriptions, which, as we have discussed, really tell us very little about teacher effectiveness, lesson quality or student learning. And because teachers will be learning from you about how to discuss and analyze instruction differently, you will need to be on your toes to provide a solid role model. Here is a fun way to practice this skill of describing through a quantitative lens.

You can do this silently or out loud (maybe this is a fun party game?). To get started, use the examples below. Your task is to describe as much as you can about these places and events using only numerically quantifiable descriptors. It may seem silly at first, but you will find after doing a few of them that your way of viewing situations changes. Look back through this chapter if you need a reminder about what kinds of numerical data you can collect, i.e., frequency, iterations, time intervals, etc.

1. Watch children on the playground for five minutes. Describe, in quantitative terms, what you see.

2. Sit in the staff lounge for five minutes. Describe what you see.

3. While grocery shopping, get busy with your quantitative analysis.

4. Listen attentively to your family or friends during a meal for five minutes. Describe what you heard using only quantifiable descriptors.

5. At your next training session, analyze the adult instruction you observe.

The Leaders Lounge

A major pillar of the coaching approach elaborated in this book is the use of accurate and specific language to describe teaching and learning. As the leader of your site or district, the way you use language profoundly influences your team. If you use mainly qualitative descriptors, then they will too. To be more specific, they will come to believe that qualitative terms are preferable when describing teaching performance, student learning, school improvement, and just about everything else on your campus.

If your goal as a leader is to improve teacher and student learning, qualitative descriptors and conclusions simply will not get you there. It can make people feel better in the short term, but in the long term it creates an environment where everybody self-certifies as a "good" teacher, that student achievement is "pretty good" and the school's performance as an organization is "fine", or "getting better".

Your focus with this exercise is to get a better handle on how you describe instruction and instructional things to your staff. To help you to hear yourself, and thus be cognizant of your tendency to use either qualitative or quantitative language when talking about teaching and learning, complete the task below. For each statement, convert it to its opposite.

Qualitative	Quantitative
1. The teaching here at our school is very solid.	1.
2. Our student scores show that most students are making good progress.	2.
3.	3. We have changed reading programs three times during the past five years, during which time student achievement in every grade has declined in each sub-group by an average of 11 percent.
4.	4. The teacher asked 14 questions of students during the 15-minute lesson observation. Of those 14 questions, six of them were responded to in complete sentences that utilized at least one of the correct academic science words listed in the lesson objective.
5. "Wow. Based on my drop-ins yesterday, these fifth-grade teachers really know how to engage students in their learning! Way to go!"	5.
6.	6. Based on 120 minutes of observation in all 10 of our fourth- through sixth-grade classrooms yesterday, 20 percent of instructional time is lost because teachers did not have materials ready.

This may have been a difficult exercise for you, but neither teachers nor grade levels nor organizations can improve when the words used to describe performance are vague, subject to interpretation and trite. Remember, people listen to you and the language you use. Make it real and you will get real improvement.

Fun Quiz

1. Acrobat is to safety net as teacher is to _____.
    a. *Pass the Pen*
    b. intervention
    c. lesson planning
    d. feedback

2. A qualitative conclusion from watching a lesson would be:
    a. "That was really good."
    b. "Students were really engaged."
    c. "Now that was powerful!"
    d. all of these

3. A quantitative way of observing instruction would utilize which terms?
    a. frequency
    b. total number of uses
    c. differentiation
    d. a and b

4. Which of the following coaching methods do not happen during instruction?
    a. *Pass the Pen*
    b. *Co-Plan/Co-Teach*
    c. *Narrated Lesson*
    d. *Real-Time Corrective Feedback*

5. Coaches are always trying to help teachers reach a level of _____ with respect to a particular behavior.
    a. dependence
    b. push
    c. independence
    d. self-certification

Chapter 9
The Methods Of Performance-Based Coaching
Part Three

Introduction

This is the final chapter that deals with the specific methods utilized in Performance-Based Coaching™. As such, it deals with two extremes of coaching, neither of which are usually addressed or even mentioned in other approaches. Indeed, we find that coaches frequently don't interact regularly with these two types of extremes for a variety of reasons. We refer here to teachers that are superstars, and those that are falling stars. Whatever terminology you prefer, these are the very good and the very bad. Our experiences and surveys show that coaches avoid — by design or by accident — working with teachers in these two camps. "How can I help someone who is so darn good?" is the question they ask themselves when confronted with a superstar. "How can I help someone who is so darn ineffective?" is the question asked when dealing with falling stars. Worry no more; the methods are just around the corner.

Objectives

In this chapter you will learn:

1. The rationale for providing coaching to both very high-performing teachers and very low-performing teachers;

2. Two specific methods for dealing with those teachers;

3. Why self-analysis and self-propelling reflection are usually more prominent among high-performers in all fields;

You Have Probably Heard Or Seen This Before

Most everyone at Geraldine Ferraro Middle School knew of "The A Team," a group of five teachers whose creativity, skill and student test scores consistently shined. They were sometimes excused from teacher trainings to work on "special projects", and teachers and administrators from other sites and districts would frequently come on campus to observe their teaching. As one new teacher at the site put it: "It only took about two days here to know that these were the giants on campus. I was genuinely afraid to talk to them for the first month."

Likewise, everyone knew who the members of "The Coffee Break Team" were and how they came to be included in that group of four teachers. By rumor and by fact, most of the faculty knew that these teachers were just plain lousy. Their students' test scores were poor, and the teachers' penchant for maximizing every minute of a break to drink coffee with each other gave rise to their collective moniker. The principal and assistant principal avoided these rooms, unsure of what to do to improve their teaching. Stephanie, the coach at the school, was sympathetic to the plight of both groups, though she followed the directive of the principal to not include members of either "team" in her regular coaching rounds. Never comfortable with that directive, Stephanie related that it was probably for the best.

Even if I had been allowed to work with those teachers, I really wasn't sure what I would do. So I didn't do anything, but I never felt good about that.

Facing Reality — Dealing With Both Ends Of The Bell Curve

It is going to happen – hopefully as infrequently as possible — that you as a coach find yourself coaching a lesson that is simply going off the rails. For a variety of reasons, the lesson is progressing in a downward spiral and you see no value for its coaching opportunities or for learning by students. As we have mentioned previously, coaches bear a responsibility for ensuring that coaching is learning time for everyone: teacher and students. But when that is no longer possible, you as the coach must intervene, and intervene strongly. Such situations call for a method known as *Resuscitation,* with no black humor or innuendo implied. The lesson simply has no footing and must be set back on a productive course.

At the other end of the extreme are those teachers who are, or who have become, exceptionally skilled at the targeted behaviors identified and worked on in previous coaching sessions. Together with their other knowledge, experience and skills, these teachers demonstrate a mastery of teaching that is fully reflective of district priorities and emphases, as well as lesson design, instructional delivery and student learning. So what are we to do as Performance-Based Coaches™ with these high fliers? Should we just excuse them from further coaching, or engage them in practicing more of the same, albeit at a high level. Recall our several vignettes and examples of high-caliber athletes, or anyone else who has reached the apogee of their field. Do they just stop learning because no one can teach them anything they don't already know and do well? Hardly. These experts seek out coaches and anyone else who can help them to see something they have missed, to try something different, or to help them to self-analyze their craft at an even higher level.

Our method for these superstars is abbreviated as *FBI*, and that stands for *Full-Bore Introspection*. While it shares the same philosophical base with the other methods discussed in this book, it is distinguished by its emphasis on having teachers articulate fully and with extreme detail, why they do what they do in the exact moment they are doing it. This would be similar to asking an expert golfer or surgeon to explain, or talk through, their actions in real time. While it may sound a bit awing, for teachers who have shown consistent levels of excellence, you will see that they find the challenge of this method to be inspiring and full of self-reflection and learning. As a Performance-Based Coach™, you will probably find it offers the same for you.

Working With High Fliers

Anytime we watch someone perform at the highest levels of expertise in a given area, most of us are simply awed by the spectacle of their skill, form and execution. We appreciate their grace, their focus and their dedication to something that has undoubtedly required thousands of hours of practice, study and commitment. Whether it is Michael Jordan shooting a basketball, an opera singer with a voice that shakes the room, or the steady hand of a world-class painter, they are among the elite and we are usually content to just admire their work with reverence and appreciation.

But what if we could actually hear them talk to us about what they do, how they do it, why they make the decisions they do, and what they wrestle with inside their collective heads? Perhaps you have listened to an expert make external the internal workings of their mind. Chances are, it was as riveting as their work, and you gained a new perspective on their craft and of their thinking processes.

Now think for a moment how we treat expert teachers. Everyone "knows" they are expert, everyone respects them for their skill and knowledge, and everyone, in their own way, pays homage to their reputation. But how often do we get to learn from them about what is going on in their head when they are in the act of teaching? Have we ever been afforded the opportunity to watch them teach, and then to boot, have them talk to us at the same time about why they do what they do? Sadly, the answer is probably "no". But that can easily be changed, and the benefits and the benefactors to hearing that thinking unveiled are manifold.

The corollary to the high performer is the absolute novice, or sometimes, the person who we describe as "challenged" to do a particular event or activity. As much as one of your humble authors wanted to play in the National Basketball Association, several factors prevented that plan from coming to fruition: too short, fundamentally unsound, and finally, lack of natural ability. That about guarantees a low performer in most anything. Though almost taboo in education to acknowledge or discuss, tit is true that there is a great deal of variance among teachers on every staff. It is usually common knowledge — though unspoken — that many students each year are assigned to teachers with a track record of poor teaching, poor self-improvement habits, and poor results with students. There, we said it. At one end of The Bell Curve of teacher competence is a group of teachers who are just plain not up to par on a daily basis. Yet, for most of their professional lives, they will be treated as all the other teachers; they will attend the same trainings, go to the same conferences and blend in. So much for differentiation of professional development opportunities.

When it comes to coaching, this group of teachers is frequently forgotten or given a pass. After all, they sometimes defend their poor practices, invoke their years of experience, or impugn the credentials of anyone who dares to provide help. Within this group, fortunately, are those who want to get better, who eagerly absorb information and willingly accept help. Coaches, both of these subsets of struggling teachers need you perhaps more than any other group of teachers on your campus.

In this chapter we address the un-addressable: what to do with high fliers and those teachers who, at least currently, can't improve or won't commit to improving?

Method #7: *Resuscitation*
Bringing A Lesson Back From The Dead

One of the most important jobs of a coach during any coaching session is to ensure that the lesson is successful. This is true regardless of the coaching method being utilized or of the teacher in front of the room. If a lesson we are coaching strays far afield of its objective, lacks any sort of coherence, or veers off into a dark abyss of confusion, false information and illogic, it is the coach's responsibility to fix it. This means that the coach steps in –for as brief a time as possible, ideally — to get the lesson back on track or to demonstrate one or more behaviors for the teacher to replicate that will resuscitate the lesson. When a coach resuscitates a lesson, they are not taking total control of the teacher's classroom for the remainder of the activity. They are only stepping in to provide a piece of the lesson that, by all available evidence at the moment, indicates that the teacher is not about to provide, or is incapable of providing.

Different than most coaching methods whereby the coach steps into and out of the lesson quickly to provide a short, clear directive, *Resuscitation* involves the coach in more than just addressing a target behavior; the coach is intervening in the gestalt of the lesson, which can sometimes require re-doing aspects of the lesson that were ineffective, omitted or unintelligble.   Logically, this method requires the coach to have formulated a way out of the lesson in such a way that the teacher can continue in a productive fashion. This is a challenging method for all parties concerned, but no useful teaching or learning happens for anyone when a lesson has lost its way.

Coaching Method Steps

1. The coach identifies, based on a mounting collection of evidence, that the lesson is no longer working.

2. The coach makes a decision that the issuance of a directive, or utilization of another coaching method, will not be sufficient to reorient the instruction.

3. The coach steps into the lesson, usually with a short phrase like, "Let me see, Mr. Clark, if I can use a couple of our target teaching behaviors in a way that helps us to refocus this lesson."

4. The coach trades places with the teacher, temporarily removing them from the lesson.

5. The coach re-teaches the portion of the lesson that was just observed and demonstrates one or more behaviors that can bring the lesson back to life.

6. The coach narrates to the teacher and students exactly what the teacher will do when he or she re-enters the lesson.

7. The coach steps out of the lesson, trading places again with the teacher.

Coaching Tip

Resuscitation is used to bring a lesson back on track and ensure that the lesson is productive for the teacher and for the students. When narrating the expectation for the teacher's re-entry into the lesson, make sure that the students and the teacher know exactly what is about to happen so that the transition is smooth and successful.

A Closer Look at Step 3
Step Back To Take Two Steps Forward – Hitting The Undo Button

- When a coach decides that a lesson has taken a turn that will lead in a direction that is unrecoverable, it is important to react quickly. However, much like hitting the "undo" button on your keyboard, it is important that you go far enough back to correct the error, but not so far back that you must re-do something that was fine from the start. Certainly, this is a big job that happens almost on the fly.

- Most often, if you as the coach believe — based on your evidence — that Resuscitation is needed, the teacher knows that something is wrong as well. *Resuscitation* gives the teacher a hand to grab when they are falling. It also resets the lesson back to a functional place so more beneficial coaching methods can be utilized.

- Think of yourself as a surgeon who has a range of skills for all of the patient conditions you may encounter. That is just a hazard of the job, but one you are prepared for. The use of this method with the same teacher more than once, however, probably means that another coaching method, like *Co-Plan/Co-Teach* would be more beneficial and would serve to overt such unpleasant and uncomfortable situations.

Resuscitation should not be used when a less invasive coaching method can accomplish the same change in behavior. Let's look at two situations when *Resuscitation* can do more harm than good.

Resuscitation is Unwarranted	The Better Method
The system of student-to-student interaction being used in the classroom is not optimal for getting students to talk to each other about the lesson content, but it doesn't inhibit the progression of the lesson.	Though a different system of student interaction may drastically impact the lesson being taught, stopping the lesson to implement it without adequate foundation can be confusing. If a current classroom structure for student discussion is ineffective but still allows the lesson to progress, schedule a *Co-Plan/Co-Teach* session to discuss in detail the desired change in structure prior to the next coaching session.
The teacher demonstrates a tendency to lecture for extended periods of time without stopping to allow students to respond or process the information. The coach wants to show the teacher how to break up their lessons and when to ask questions.	If pacing or lesson segmentation are keeping the teacher from eliciting student language production, taking over the lesson through *Resuscitation* will not help the teacher learn how to better pace instruction. Instead, *Real-Time Corrective Feedback* should be used to step in at a given time interval, or at strategic points during the teacher's lecture, to prompt them to pause and ask questions.

Resuscitation is most frequently needed because of two distinct and observable situations. Let's take a look at how *Resuscitation* makes an immediate and positive impact.

Resuscitation is Needed	How to Transition Back into the Lesson
The system of student-to-student or student-to-teacher interaction has broken down to the point that the lesson is not progressing, and classroom management has become the focus of instruction.	Stop the lesson and teach the students the system of interaction that you expect, writing the steps on the board as you teach them. Go back to the last point in the lesson that was effective and ask again the questions using the new system. Once the lesson is progressing, pose a question to the group. During the discussion, transition the teacher back into the lesson. Leave the steps written on the board for reference.
It has become apparent that the outcome the teacher is expecting from students is either inaccurate or divergent from grade-level/content expectations. Most frequently, the teacher has not personally read the text being discussed or has stated several inaccuracies about the content being taught.	When it becomes obvious that a teacher does not have mastery of their content, it is important to stop the lesson and intervene. In this case, the coach can either adjust the objective of the lesson or switch the focus to a review of a prior concept that the teacher is able to navigate. A third option is to limit the remainder of the lesson to what the teacher does know correctly. Either way, a *Co-Plan/Co-Teach* session should be scheduled prior to the next coaching session to go over the concepts necessary to effectively teach the lesson.

Resuscitation is a method that challenges the assumptions of the teacher in the classroom. Most teachers who find themselves in need of *Resuscitation* probably thought that their current systems of lesson planning, content mastery or instruction were acceptable or efficient. Having your assumptions called into question is rarely welcomed and seldom enjoyed. However, challenging a set of deeply rooted assumptions is one of the most important steps for initiating a lasting behavioral change.

Though having to step in to fully take over a lesson that has fallen off track is rare, keep in mind that it can often lead to rapid and drastic improvement for a teacher. After all, if the lesson was ineffective while the coach was present, imagine how many times lessons may have failed when you weren't there. In many cases, the teacher –and frequently, the students — know this to be true

Much like having a doctor tell you that your blood pressure is too high, or going to buy new jeans only to find out that you need a larger size, the change comes from what is done after the *Resuscitation*, not from the *Resuscitation* itself. Always schedule a *Co-Plan/Co-Teach* session prior to your next in-class session and never end a coaching cycle when *Resuscitation* is utilized.

Who Benefits the Most from *Resuscitation*?		
Teacher Experience	Overall Skill Level	Level of Independence
Rarely used for teachers with greater levels of experience, as they are usually savvy enough to steer lessons toward things that have worked in the past. More frequently used for teachers with little to no experience, as misconceptions that have a greater impact on the lesson's success are more common.	Rarely used for teachers with greater levels of skill, as they are usually able to correct lesson missteps with less invasive methods. More effective for teachers with lower skill levels to ensure that lessons stay on track and can be completed successfully.	*Resuscitation* does not support the development of independence as a skill and should therefore be used only when absolutely necessary.

Method #8: Full-Bore Introspection (FBI)
When The Goal Is Better Than The Best

As discussed in the introduction to these final two methods, some teachers are simply off the charts in their ability to implement and integrate new behaviors and skills into their teaching inventories. In many cases, they are their own best "coach", and possess the ability to both teach and to watch and analyze their teaching simultaneously. Certainly, these teachers are few and far between, but that doesn't mean we as Performance-Based Coaches™ shouldn't be ready to assist them in their continuing growth.

Paradoxically, *FBI* requires in many ways a higher level of instructional analysis and intervention for the coach than most of the other methods. Here's why: the role of the coach during an *FBI* coaching session is to identify in real-time (as the teacher is teaching) visible or verbal evidence of a teacher behavior that is implemented perfectly for the benefit of students' learning. Imagine it happening like this: you are watching Mr. Tokhi teach and he consistently utilizes a specific verbal command to students that elicits from them academic-sounding complete sentence answers. At that moment when the coach sees Mr. Tokhi' behavior, the coach signals to Mr. Tokhi to stop teaching and respond to the coach's "invitation to analyze." The coach verbally directs to Mr. Tokhi the following invitation:

Please articulate your thought process that led to phrasing your last three questions to students in a way that elicited the academic complete sentences they produced?

Mr. Tokhi, familiar with the protocol for using the *FBI* method, pauses and then discusses for 30-45 seconds his thinking. Of course, students are hearing his answers as well, so it is a good idea to give a short description to the students of how this process will work before starting. It is common for students of teachers who have been regularly coached to quickly see that this looks like just another version of what they have seen before when coaches and teachers work collaboratively to improve their instruction.

There are no limits to the number of times the coach can "invite" a teacher to elucidate his or her thinking about a behavior they have implemented. But for this method to be maximally effective, it requires a coach who is skilled at "seeing ahead" of the lesson. By this we mean a coach who can foreshadow where a teacher is going and what observable behavior is likely to occur. Because the intervention in this method is related to the skillful analysis and probing of the teacher's thinking by the coach, there is no need to tell the teacher what you will be looking for ahead of time. After all, their teaching and your interventions (read: invitations to display thinking) will be in real time in the most absolute sense of the term.

Most importantly, the real-time articulation of invisible thought processes can get teacher's thinking about — and re-thinking — the way they teach *during* the act of instruction. This re-thinking often leads to realizations about how and why their current practices are effective, as well as how he or she might innovate their practice further. The true power of this method lies in the dynamic interplay between insightful invitations to analyze by the coach, and the fresh, uncensored thinking-into-words by the teacher.

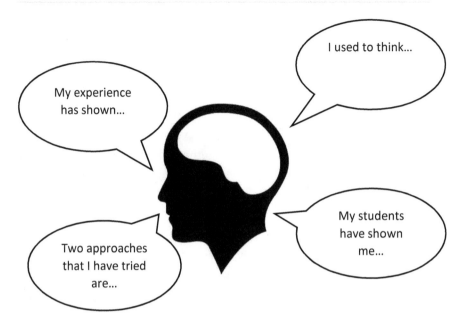

Coaching Method Steps

1. Select the teacher and explain the method, especially why you
    think it will be beneficial to them.

2. Make clear that the focus of this method is for the teacher to
    articulate his or her thinking – not for the coach, but for
    themselves. The coach is just the "intervener".

3. The coach seats himself or herself in a place near the teacher,
    but there is no need to be as close to the teacher as some
    other methods require.

4. Establish with the teacher a signal by which the coach will
    intervene.

5. Explain that there is no time limit to the teacher's comments,
    although good sense should dictate.

6. The coach "intervenes" as provocative or interesting events in the lesson arise as the result of a specific behavior by the teacher. The coach "invites" verbal analysis from the teacher.

7. It is frequently a desire of teachers to have a post-conference with the coach to "stitch together" the various explanations and analyses. For this reason, the coach may want to jot some notes.

A Closer Look At Step 6
Inviting Teachers to Display Their Thinking

The role of the coach at this lynchpin step of the method is to "invite" a teacher to verbally analyze and reflect on a very recent behavior. But an *invitation to talk* is not the same as a question. Let's look at this in more detail, first with a simple example, and then with some from actual *FBI* coach-teacher interactions.

Scenario A

You run into a fellow teacher at the store who you know only through some occasional staff lounge conversations. You know, however, that this person recently returned from a trip to Europe. You are likely, based on your collegial relationship, to ask a question like this:

"How was your trip to Europe?"

Recognizing your question as one that usually comes from an acquaintance, and not a close friend, the fellow teacher responds like this:

"It was great. We had lots of fun and learned a ton."

Congratulations! You both played your parts perfectly. A simple question was asked, and a simple answer was given. And everyone is
happy. Now compare the following scenario with the same facts, except that both teachers are close friends.

Scenario B

> "Diane, welcome back. Tell me all about your trip."

> "Well, we left from San Francisco late at night, and we were so excited that we almost forgot to put the suitcases in the car, but we…"

In the second example, Friend 1 "invited" Friend 2 to really talk about the trip. As a result, both the quantity of Friend 2's answers and the details were far greater. This is an example of why *FBI* relies on the skillful formation of "invitations" by the coach to the teacher, and not merely the phrasing of simple questions. Look at the examples below.

Questions Start With These Kinds of Words	Invitations Start With These Kinds of Words
Who, What, When, Where, Why, How	*Describe, Detail, Articulate, Explain, Discuss, Compare, Contrast, Say more about, Talk me through, Help me to understand, Please tell me about…*
What did you do with students just now?	**Detail** your thinking about why you focused your questions on three specific students?
Why are you repeating the objective three times?	**Explain** the evidence you rely on to determine when to repeat the objective?
When do you select students to speak orally?	**Discuss** the criteria you just used for selecting students to respond orally?

Remember these three things to get this method right. First, all of the coach's *invitations* are centered on observable teacher behaviors. That means you can either hear it or see it. Be careful to not get caught up in asking questions about process, i.e., What system are you using to maximize student engagement? Those process questions are characteristic of low-impact lesson analysis and coaching approaches that do almost nothing to help teachers improve their craft. Second, remember that short questions beget short, usually vacant, answers. Invitations elicit more of everything: content, analysis, detail and collaboratively-mediated growth. Finally, approach this method with enthusiasm and curiosity. That is the opportunity we are giving teachers when we skillfully use *Full-Bore Introspection*.

Things To Ponder Or Discuss

1. Think of at least three "experts" (in your choice of field, endeavor or specialty) and discuss why you would find their "open mind" discussions fascinating.

2. Why do we tend to neglect those at the high and low ends of the teaching spectrum when it comes to specialized learning opportunities?

3. Describe your enthusiasm or apprehension about working with teachers who find themselves in the lower range of competence.

4. As a teacher, discuss your excitement (or not) about having a coach come into your classroom to use the *Full-Bore Introspection* method.

5. Identify three specific ways that the use of *Resuscitation* might actually be a catalyst for a teacher to improve.

6. Elaborate on your reaction to learning about the differences between a question and an "invitation" to talk.

The Coaches Corner

This chapter is likely to have produced in your reactions or feelings of both excitement and trepidation. How wonderful to hear an expert teacher elucidate his or her thinking while in the dynamic process of teaching! How nervous I might be if I identify that a lesson has lost its way and it is my job to resuscitate it. From our interviews of hundreds of instructional coaches, the reality is that the bulk of your practice will not involve the use of either of these methods. Still, it is likely that at some point you will need them. So, what can you do to prepare for either of these eventualities? Here are three ways you can be ready.

1. Prepare at least two scripts that you can use if and when you need to assume control of a lesson per the steps in *Resuscitation*. By having two well-thought-out (and even rehearsed) ways of verbally excusing the teacher from the lesson, you will be in a better place to right the ship and get students learning before passing the tiller back to the teacher. Review the examples in this chapter if that gives you some ideas. You will have plenty on your mind when using this method; don't let a temporary loss for words be a stumbling block.

2. Using invisible ink, lock yourself in a sealed vault in a remote underground outpost and write the names of three teachers you have known in your career who you believe would fall into the category of "low performer". For each of them, write some adjectives (words that describe) that describe what you know, or think you know, about their approach to improvement. For example, we could describe teacher

Sergio as non-energetic, negative and jaded when it comes to improving himself as a teacher. Yes, this is a tough exercise, but it will help you to focus your choice of coaching methods when you work with these kinds of teachers.

3. Now write the names of three outstanding teachers you have known or experienced. Using the list of "invitation" words presented in this chapter (or use others that you may find), craft three invitations for each teacher to share their thinking processes about something they do that you find interesting. Have fun with this, but take seriously your learning with respect to the differences between questions and invitations. Who knows? Maybe you will actually be able to utilize *FBI* with them sometime.

The Leaders Lounge

This chapter deals with a topic that seems off-limits in most educational institutions — the fact that both ends of The Bell Curve exist on our faculties in the form of outstanding teachers or underwhelming teachers. Probably more than any other person at your site, with the possible exception of your coach or coaches, you know and have witnessed the "performance variance" between teachers at your site. You know that in many cases a large portion of a student's likely level of academic achievement will owe to the competence of the teacher to which he or she is assigned. Performance-Based Coaching™ is not a miracle, but it has shown a strong track record of success in working with these low performers. But for this type of coaching to be effective requires that you, as the site or district leader, work with your coach to properly and accurately diagnose and group teachers for their work with your coach. Here is a system we have successfully used across the country to group teachers for coaching and to describe their improvement over time.

Fliers

These are teachers whose performance is almost always stellar and getting even better. They relish new ideas, approaches and methods, and are the first to try things and work them out fully. They're not the flashiest or the loudest, but you know that when you open the door to their classroom — regardless of the day or time — students will be learning, and you will be impressed.

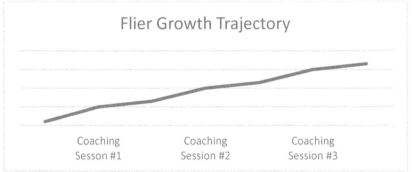

Tryers

These teachers demonstrate with their words and actions that they take seriously their effectiveness and on-going professional growth. They may struggle initially with new ideas and methods, but they persevere until they get it right. They are usually upbeat and realistic about their current strengths and areas of need. Moreover, they are usually appreciative of assistance and avail themselves regularly of learning opportunities. They seem to know that getting better requires consistent effort and practice.

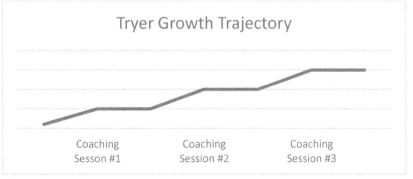

Cant's

For a variety of reasons, teachers who qualify for placement in this group seem to struggle with new ideas, approaches or requirements. They find that their repertoire of skills is sometimes insufficient for providing students with consistently high-quality instruction. Most indicative of this group is that the rate and depth of their improvement is less than is necessary to get the job done correctly. They usually need extra explanation, detail and assistance to properly implement or improve their skills.

Won'ts

This group of teachers is defined by their predictable resistance to new ideas or approaches or their unwillingness to practice something until they become proficient. In some cases, members of this group are vocal about their lack of desire to improve. In other cases, their public verbal comments would seem to describe a level of competence that their actual classroom histories do not bear out. Some can be quite outgoing in their defiance with respect to improving their teaching knowledge and skills.

Clearly, discussions of this type are something that require a great deal of care, integrity and professionalism. But if we group students for specific types of instruction based on identifiable and measurable needs, why have we resisted this practice for so many years with teachers? Why do we pretend that teachers can't be grouped in terms of their professional competence? To change a school's or district's performance requires improving the performance of its members — all of its members. Maybe you remember the bad joke at the beginning of this book.

How do you move a cemetery?

Answer: *One body at a time.*

Fun Quiz

1. This chapter deals with coaching teachers at both ends of the _____ _____.
    a. scenery
    b. Bell Curve
    c. spectrum
    d. educational landscape

2. The verb *to resuscitate* is defined in the dictionary as:
    a. to revive
    b. to revitalize
    c. to re-do
    d. a and b

3. The coaching method *FBI* is to thinking as invitation is to _____.
    a. response
    b. rationalization
    c. party
    d. fun

4. High achievers in most arenas look to coaches and others to _____ their thinking and performance possibilities.
    a. refine
    b. expand
    c. consolidate
    d. affirm

5. Do you believe most high-performing teachers know they are high performing?

    Yes   No   Not Sure

Chapter 10
Building Teacher Independence

Introduction

As you have seen, each of the coaching methods, though all slightly different in their implementation, have at their core the active nature of real-time feedback and a focus on performance by correcting or enhancing the use of a targeted behavior. Every teacher throughout their individual coaching cycles will experience a different combination and ratio of coaching methods. One teacher may complete an entire coaching cycle and make impressive growth in their practice through the sole use of *Pass the Pen*, while another teacher may experience three or four different methods that do not include *Pass the Pen* at all.

Though all these methods focus on the skillful use of a targeted behavior, the ultimate outcome of the entire coaching process is the creation of what we call a "strategically innovative" teacher. By this, we mean teachers who consistently and independently implement instruction using a common set of highly effective behaviors and practices. They are innovative in their use of specific skills and methods across all areas of their instruction, frequently in ways that go far beyond what was mastered with the assistance of coaching. That they are able to sustain the use of these behaviors is critical for organizational capacity building and the minimization of teacher performance variance across classrooms, grade levels, and schools. This chapter addresses the dynamics of organizing and implementing coaching methods to bring about teacher independence.

Objectives

In this chapter you will learn:

1. That a behavior cannot be considered mastered if its implementation requires support from a coach;

2. That independence is the outcome of a systematic process, and is not usually a natural occurrence;

3. That neglecting any of the phases of independence can hinder the development of new behaviors;

4. Why the ultimate outcome of a skillfully implemented coaching effort is a teacher who can independently sustain a behavior and strategically innovate within their practice.

You've Probably Seen Or Heard This Before

The entire staff of Bella Vista Junior High School is assembled in the cafeteria to kick off the new school year. Almost 40 teachers in number, the school is a place that few teachers leave and where a feeling of family is part of its culture. The principal, Ms. Fender, has been at the school for almost 10 years and is well-regarded by her staff for her organizational skills and the emphasis she places on frequent professional development opportunities. The teachers know that the next two days will be dedicated to learning about a new writing-across-the curriculum program, as well as department meetings dedicated to reviewing new instructional materials. While most teachers are upbeat, everyone feels the aftermath of a critical series of articles in the local newspaper over the summer describing the school's steady decline in student test scores. Once the flagship school of the district, more parents are opting to drive their students to a school across town that shows higher student performance.

A consultant has been invited to address the staff for the first part of the day. Ms. Fender states in her welcoming remarks that she is confounded as to why student achievement is declining, especially in light of the staff's aggressive professional development efforts over the past five years. The consultant introduces herself and quickly asks all teachers to list as many programs, initiatives, methods and strategies they can remember being asked to implement during that time period. Teachers are then asked to share these with the whole group. The list swells to 35 different topics: character building, write-to-read, Silent Sustained Reading, one-to-one devices, instructional differentiation, cooperative learning, flex scheduling, math facts focus, power vocabulary, new science and social science curriculums, student peer learning partners, cognitive coaching, Homework Club, and the list went on.

The various topics cover almost the entire chart paper. The consultant then asks a question that elicits more than a few gasps: "Put an X on your paper by the ones you still implement on a daily basis at what you would consider a high level of competence." After a few minutes, the consultant asks teachers to share their lists among the members of their table groups. We listen in on one of those groups.

Pam: "Let's start with instructional differentiation. I think we did that last summer. Do you all remember that one?"

Dave: "That just didn't seem to work for me. It was too structured. But I did like the power vocabulary program. I still use that."

Rick: "I don't really think either of those were good for our kids, although the differentiation strategies were good. I used to do them a lot when Peggy was coaching us on them. Now I focus a lot on homework, so I thought Homework Club would work, but I was the only social science teacher who had kids design their own homework assignments like they showed us how to do."

Shelly: "I just didn't have time to prepare the homework sheets like the trainer showed us. And my students didn't really turn them in. I still do the power vocabulary strategies, but only twice a week."

Pam: "Does anybody still do the write-to-read stuff we learned about that one year?"

By the end of the morning, the consultant had led the group to craft a concluding paragraph that accurately and succinctly summed up the outcomes of their five years' worth of professional development. It was hard for the staff to craft, and even harder to read, but only a few teachers disagreed that it was a true conclusion.

> *We have implemented many programs and ideas over the past five years with the goal of improving instruction and student learning. But our implementation of those programs, initiatives and strategies is random, and most teachers pick and choose what they want to use.*

The consultant concluded by asking the staff to consider one more question for discussion after lunch.

> *"How much of your declining student achievement do you believe can be explained by this statement?"*

Is Change Optional?

We can see from this real-life example that even well-intentioned school leaders and teachers sometimes fail in their efforts to improve things. But if we analyze the root cause of their failure, the fault rarely can be found in the program, initiative or strategy itself. Instead, four phenomena play out over and over again in schools and districts that lead to the concluding statement written by the staff at Bella Vista Junior High School.

1. We take on too many initiatives.

2. We forget that each initiative brings with it – even if we don't acknowledge it — a list of new teacher behaviors to be learned, and old behaviors to be discarded.

3. We don't properly assist teachers in the classroom to achieve independent mastery of new behaviors.

4. We pay little to no attention to a teacher's ability to sustain a mastered behavior over time.

The typical result of these factors in most places is just what we heard from the staff at the junior high school above: most innovations are implemented by only a few teachers, they are substantially modified, or they are discarded. In sum, behavioral change is optional. And when change is optional, improvement is optional. And when improvement is optional, then school improvement is practically impossible. This is an example of a negative reinforcing loop, as you may recall from a previous chapter. Our failure or resistance to change brings about lower organizational performance, which in turn brings about more failure and resistance to change. Fortunately, we can end this cycle by making behavioral change less of an option by coaching teachers in their own classrooms to master new and desirable behaviors. When we create and use the structured process laid out in this chapter we can maximize the probability of a teacher being able to sustain a given behavior at a high level.

Another View Of Building — Or Not Building — Independence And Sustainability

Not surprisingly, most teachers would be quick to agree that helping students gain independent control of new knowledge, behaviors and skills is highly desirable, if not critical, in today's results-driven educational milieu. Here is a short classroom example to see another perspective on building independence and sustainability.

Ms. Kady, a fifth-grade math teacher in Flagstaff, Arizona, has just finished demonstrating how to solve a multi-step algebra problem to find the value of an unknown variable. She has asked her students to attempt solving a similar problem with a partner as she walks around the room to offer support. At the first table, Ms. Kady is met with a pair of students who have nothing written yet on their paper.

Students	Ms. Kady
"I don't know what to do."	
	"Remember to use inverse operations."
(The students pause and look blankly at the problem.)	
	"Since the problem says +2 on the left side, you will need to subtract the 2 from both sides."
(The students write -2 on their paper.)	
	"You will have to subtract the two from each side of the equation."

The conversation continues, with Ms. Kady telling the students each step of the problem. At each step, errors are made that need to be corrected. After several minutes the students complete the problem and it is correct, but they are unable to complete a single aspect of the skill correctly, even with the support of their teacher.

The second group of students that Ms. Kady visits has not yet begun working on the problem.

Students	Ms. Kady
"What do we do?"	
	"Remember to use inverse operations."
"Oh…yeah."	
(The students subtract two from both sides of the equation and continue to solve the problem.)	
	"Perfect! You got it."

As Ms. Kady walks away, the students look at the next problem and then their hands shoot up immediately. They patiently wait for Ms. Kady to come back to offer more support. These students would be able to complete every problem as long as the teacher was able to provide continuous support for every aspect of the targeted skill.

As Ms. Kady approaches the third group, she sees that they have also written down the equation but have not yet begun to solve the problem.

Students	Ms. Kady
"Ms. Kady, We need help!"	
	"What do you need help with?"
"We need to subtract two from both sides of the problem, right?"	
	"Yes! That's right."
"OK. Thanks!"	

The students quickly finish the problem and move on to the next one. Despite having known how to complete the problem correctly, the students lack the confidence to try the next problem without checking to see if they are on the right track. As Ms. Kady walks away, their hands raise into the air.

Ms. Kady approaches the fourth table to see that the students there have moved quickly through three problems and are working on solving a fourth.

Students	Ms. Kady
"This is easy!" "Why? We did that one already. $X = -4$." "OK. Thanks!" "Ohhh…Oops!"	"How is it going over here?" "Well that's good. You might want to go back and check number three." "You are close, but go back and check your second step. You added two, but you forgot to use the inverse of the operation."

The students fix the error and begin solving the other problems on their own. As Ms. Kady approaches the fifth and final group, she sees that the students have completed the same number of problems as the last group.

Students	Ms. Kady
  "I hate fractions. I didn't want to divide both sides by ½ so I changed it to 0.5 before I started the problem." "Thanks!"	"That's interesting. Explain to me what you did here on number five." "Well, it would be good for you to practice working with fractions, but that is one way to solve the problem."

The students in the group continue working on their own. They make few to no errors, often by appropriately changing some of the more difficult problems into forms with which they are more comfortable with. When Ms. Kady moves back to the front of the room, she has worked directly with each group. Many of the groups were not able to implement the target skill at the outset on their own, but they were able to use the given skill to complete the task while she was helping them. One of the groups did not rely on Ms. Kady at all, instead, they made use of other independently controlled strategies to navigate the problem.

This classroom example shows us a parallel occurrence that happens in coaching. Our end goal for teachers as Performance-Based Coaches™ is for them to independently control a behavior to a level where they use it correctly and strategically without external support. You may recall from a previous chapter we defined coaching as three separate, but related, elements: *Define* terms (D), *Intervene* in the teaching (I), and *Generalize* (G). We shorthanded these to *D.I.G.* The final term, generalize, calls for the behaviors gained though coaching to be generalized to other instructional areas and times without the presence of the coach. Reflecting on our math classroom example above, Ms. Kady would be wrong to conclude that all students, since they got the right answer, have mastered the skill. Remember that four of the five groups required real-time teacher support to solve the problems. An analogous scenario occurs with coaches and leads to a common coaching error: a teacher uses a new behavior correctly during a coaching session, and the coach — and sometimes the teacher too — erroneously conclude that the skill has been mastered.

Continuum Of Interdependence

Just like Ms. Kady's math groups, teachers demonstrate certain characteristics related to independence and interdependence that are useful for Performance-Based Coaches™ to understand and use to prescribe the best coaching interventions throughout a coaching cycle. The graphic below shows what we call the Continuum of Interdependence™ and its related descriptors.

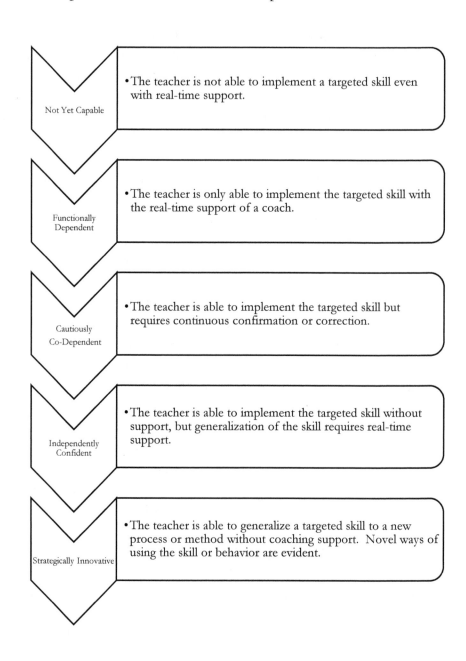

Not Yet Capable
- The teacher is not able to implement a targeted skill even with real-time support.

Functionally Dependent
- The teacher is only able to implement the targeted skill with the real-time support of a coach.

Cautiously Co-Dependent
- The teacher is able to implement the targeted skill but requires continuous confirmation or correction.

Independently Confident
- The teacher is able to implement the targeted skill without support, but generalization of the skill requires real-time support.

Strategically Innovative
- The teacher is able to generalize a targeted skill to a new process or method without coaching support. Novel ways of using the skill or behavior are evident.

Independence: The Bull's-Eye Of Performance-Based Coaching

Think about the first time you tried to use a new skill or do an activity for the first time. Did you find yourself re-reading a set of directions, or guidebook, trying to make sense of what exactly you were supposed to do? Did you find yourself going back to those directions again and again to double- and triple-check what you should do next? Did you try to do something differently than the directions specified, only to find out that it wouldn't work that way? If you are like most people, then the answer is yes to all of these.

To better understand the Continuum of Interdependence™, let's look at it through the lens of a teacher who is learning how to use a new reading curriculum. At first, the pallet of boxes, posters, books of all sizes, teacher's editions, reproducible masters, computer disks and fashionable shoulder bags and key rings seems exciting, colorful and alluring in its presentation. Not knowing how they all fit together, our teacher begins to feel overwhelmed, stranded on an island of shiny new materials sealed in impenetrable plastic. At this point, even with all of the resources in front of her, the teacher is not yet capable of implementing the program. Instead of viewing the plethora of materials like a giant and glorious Christmas present, the teacher finds herself overwhelmed. With no guidance from someone more skilled with these materials, she is likely to begin "implementation" of the program by picking and choosing among the materials for what feels comfortable, or bears some similarity to something she has previously used. The alternative option is for her to rush headlong into the full array of materials, creating a complicated and incoherent blend that would likely frustrate students and confound those who arranged for the purchase of this wonderful Christmas gift. At this point, our teacher is clearly in the *Not Yet Capable* stage of the continuum.

But with support from a trained and skillful coach, her progress through the Continuum of Interdependence™ can be planned and managed. Most teachers, whether it be with new materials, new content or new methods, can be moved from the *Not Yet Capable* box to the *Functionally Dependent* box just by the coach selecting for them an area of focus. The teacher instantly feels relieved with the narrowed focus and her initial use of the materials is far more successful than had she received no support.

Then the emails begin. Weekly, or even daily, requests for the coach to tell the teacher what to teach next begin to pile up. All too often, coaches get pulled into this sticky web, forever telling teachers what to teach next. The result of this cycle is the teacher stays at a state of functional dependence. Though such "help" allows the teacher to achieve a basic level of success, the coach must push the teacher to a higher level of independence, though she still lacks confidence and the skills necessary for effective use of the reading program.

This is the time for the coach to select interventions that move the teacher to the stage of *Cautiously Co-Dependent*. At this phase, the coach turns the conversation around, saying: "You decide what you will teach next and we can talk about it before you teach the lesson." At the stage of *Cautiously Co-Dependent.*, the teacher still needs the coach; not to tell him or her what to do, but to make sure that what he or she plans to do is correct before they try it on their own.

But the emails keep coming. The teacher is planning her own instruction but is regularly requesting coach pre-approval. It is time for the coach to push again in order to move the teacher to a level of *Independently Confident* by asking the teacher to implement her own instructional plan, after which the coach will discuss the outcomes with her. Though hesitant, the teacher attempts the lesson without real-time coaching support and finds that she was indeed able to work successfully without a safety net. There are two key points to this stage of the continuum: first, the teacher implemented the behavior with no real-time support, and second, she implemented the behavior exactly the way she had practiced it during previous coaching sessions. Our teacher now knows enough about the reading program to begin asking questions characteristic of teachers approaching the *Strategically Innovative* stage of the continuum: "How else could I use this program more effectively?"

This same Continuum of Interdependence™ applies to gaining mastery of any behavior or skill. Let's go back to Ms. Kady's classroom. There is an obvious need to move students along the continuum so that they are better able to implement new skills on their own after the teacher's support has been removed. After all, this type of real-time support is not available to students during state and national assessments, nor during the great majority of their schooling life. Teachers who neglect to focus on the progression toward independence are often blindsided by lower-than-expected test results, often stating that they don't understand how the students could have performed so poorly on a given assessment when they were able to do it in class. The same is true for teachers learning new behaviors: until they have reached the apogee of the continuum, the active intervention of a skilled coach is both the engine and the prescription for true independence.

The Value Of Each Step

Now that we have established the critical importance of moving teachers toward independence and even beyond to Strategically Innovative, let's dig deeper into the nuances of each phase and the implications for Performance-Based Coaches™.

The development of independence must be observed over time and across a variety of teaching and learning contexts, i.e., subject areas, times of day, or class composition. As coaches, we know that the teachers we work with have earned degrees and hold certifications related to their training, specializations and experience. Due to this unique intersection of factors, independence is often either assumed to be an already achieved aspect of teachers' professional preparation or experience, or as something that can be easily achieved with a quick demonstration or short in-service training. Perhaps most alarming is when teachers have spent time at a school or in a district where "self-certification" of expert competence is accepted. By simply stating, "I already know that," or "I already do that," or "I've always done that", their expert status and proclamations of independence go unchallenged. This is a slippery slope, since most of us are less-than-objective arbiters of our own talents, beauty or intelligence, among other things. Skipping over any of these phases — and the learning inherent in each of them — is both detrimental to the development of new and more effective teacher behaviors and to the organizational definition and conceptualization of what is meant by the term "teacher development". The graphic below highlights some of the risks of skipping stages by summarizing the work to be done at each phase of the continuum.

Phase on the Continuum	What If It's Skipped?	What Is Gained Here?
Not Yet Capable	The teacher feels stuck in this phase. If pushed too quickly out of this phase, early failures will solidify a belief that the targeted skill is ineffective, un-needed or impossible. Coaching may be blamed for the failure.	This phase provides an initial success for most teachers and can often challenge the assumptions a teacher has about what they or their students are capable of doing. This phase also builds quick credibility for coaches and coaching.
Functionally Dependent	As the skill is still relatively new, if pushed too quickly teachers will often unknowingly eliminate or adjust vital aspects of the skill due to time or past practice. They may also see coaching as a one-time, or drive-by, process.	This phase allows the teacher to practice the behavior correctly so that new habits form and the new skill begins to feel more natural. This phase also is useful for forging solid coaching relationships that can endure over time.

Phase on the Continuum	What If It's Skipped?	What Is Gained Here?
Cautiously Co-Dependent	The teacher has now connected the success of the skill to the assistance and interventions of the coach. If pushed too quickly, teachers will often discontinue using the skill outside of coaching sessions. Coaching can be seen as a stimulus-response interaction: coach comes, teacher performs.	This phase allows the teacher to build confidence that they have an accurate understanding and use of the target behavior. Teachers in this stage frequently desire more intensive coaching methods to accelerate their development and expertise.
Confidently Independent	The teacher now demonstrates mastery or near-mastery of the behavior or skill. They may refrain from seeking coaching support, relying on their own self-determined expertise. If pushed too quickly, the teacher can fossilize inefficient aspects of the targeted skill and become frustrated when the skill needs to be targeted again in the future.	This phase allows the coach to fine-tune a teacher's practice in a variety of contexts, since the teacher is able to implement the behavior without the coach present. This phase also builds the teacher's understanding of which aspects of the skill are the most critical to its efficient implementation and which aspects could be adjusted based on the needs of a given situation.
Strategically Innovative	This phase is the goal and apogee of the coaching process. The greatest struggle here is when other teachers overlook the time and effort that went into a teacher reaching this point. This also can be confused with being "done" with coaching: "I already did that coaching thing."	This phase brings about the greatest positive impact on student achievement, as the teacher is now able to use a collection of effective behaviors across all subject areas and can innovate their use for specific student needs.

Each of these phases provides a unique opportunity to enhance the level of sophistication a teacher is able to achieve with a given behavior. Planning and executing coaching interventions that move teachers along the Continuum of Interdependence™ constitute some of the most difficult — but vital — skills that a Performance-Based Coach™ must develop. As you design coaching cycles, it is helpful to focus on two elements for each interaction you have with a teacher: the targeted behavior the teacher is working on, and the teacher's current place on the continuum. Knowing that independence is always the overarching goal of coaching will help you to keep these two elements always in your mind. In simple terms, you are responsible for picking the trail and then coaching your teacher up the mountain to independence and, ultimately, to the peak of strategic innovation.

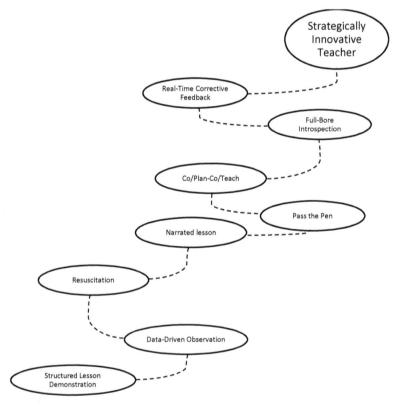

In the next chapter we will look more deeply at a coaching cycle in a very logistically focused manner. What does a typical week involve for a Performance-Based Coach™? How many teachers can be coached simultaneously? How long does a cycle last? How much of my day should be spent in classrooms? When do I have time to formulate all of these plans? Will I have some time for thinking? Where does my own professional development as a coach fit in? These questions and many more will be addressed as we look forward to learning about The Coaching Clock™.

Things To Ponder Or Discuss

1. How might the Continuum of Interdependence™ help explain why almost 48% of new teachers leave teaching after two years?

2. Do you believe your assessment as a coach of where a teacher is on the continuum will be the same as they self-determine?

3. Describe other continuums you have used professionally or personally and their effect on monitoring progress and learning.

4. Teachers should be regularly informed of a coach's assessment of where they are on the Continuum of Interdependence™. What do you think?

5. The teachers of Bella Vista Middle School listed 35 programs and initiatives over a five-year period. How many would be on your school's or district's list?

6. Most schools are places where behavioral change is optional and acceptable.

    Agree   Disagree   Not Sure

The Coaches Corner

Without a doubt, continuums used incorrectly can serve to trivialize or simplify the mastery of complex skills and behaviors. For a variety of reasons, they are sometimes viewed as grades are on a report card. A careful reading, however, of the content and purpose of our Continuum of Interdependence™ shows that it serves mainly as a tool for Performance-Based Coaches™ to chart the forward progress of the teachers with whom we work. Used in conjunction with the coaching methods described in prior chapters, they provide coaches with both a micro (daily classroom work) and a macro (progress along the continuum) view of a teacher's behavioral growth. Add in a coach's scope and assessment of school-wide, or district-wide, behavioral improvement, and you have a very complete evaluation framework for your efforts as a coach, and for the totality of your coaching program.

There are two parts to this task, the first of which asks you to do something that you probably incipiently did while reading this chapter. The second task is one that you may be asked to do, and if not, you should consider volunteering to do it. It is that important.

Task 1: Take another look at the Continuum of Interdependence™, but this time, apply it to your progress as a Performance-Based Coach™. Where are you currently? Where did you start? What are the seminal events or learnings that moved you from one phase to another? What other insights can you take from the continuum and apply to your role and continued growth as a professional coach?

Task 2: You are going to make a 15-minute presentation to your board of education. They are interested in learning about the impact Performance-Based Coaching™ has made at your school, or in your district. Use the three metrics described at the beginning of this section to design your report. Armed with this summary, look for as many places as possible to share this information: staff meetings, parent groups, community organizations, local staff development co-ops, or civic groups in your community. You alone as coach have probably the keenest and most accurate view of instructional performance at your school or in your district of anyone. Go forth and use that knowledge for good.

The Leaders Lounge

Candy has been hired as a new coach. As the school principal, you know that coaching has been tried at your site years ago and that it ended poorly. Teachers did not understand the process, the outcomes or the role of the coach.

Knowing what you know now after reading this far through the book, list here five behaviors (remember, these are either visible or audible) that you will do to ensure Candy's job yields the returns you desire, that your students need, and the expenditure of precious funds demands.

1.

2.

3.

4.

5.

Fun Quiz

1. Teachers can move through the Continuum of Interdependence™ at a consistent rate?
   a. true
   b. false
   c. not sure

2. Mastering a skill takes priority over developing independence.
   a. true
   b. false
   c. not sure

3. Coaching cycles should _____ push teachers toward independence.
   a. always
   b. sometimes
   c. never
   d. frequently

4. Independence is directly correlated with experience.

   True   False   Not Sure

5. Teachers should be allowed to innovate or adjust their practice before developing an effective level of skill regarding that practice.
   a. always
   b. sometimes
   c. never
   d. depends

Chapter 11
The Coaching Clock

Introduction

As we round the corner into the home stretch, we can summarize a bit. We have addressed the way people hear change and how to help them change. We learned eight separate and specific methods of Performance-Based Coaching™ to use when we work with teachers in real time to accelerate their development of specific behaviors. We know that our goal as coaches is to design and implement coaching cycles that lead teachers to a state of independence, or ideally, to a level of strategic innovation. Now let's turn our attention to the treatment of one of the most important, non-recurring resources a coach has: time.

Objectives

In this chapter you will learn:

1. Why coaching is a systematic progression that can and should be replicated throughout the year;

2. How each coaching cycle is guided by a set of fixed steps;

3. How the use of The Coaching Clock™ to allocate your time and activities will exponentially amplify your effectiveness;

4. Why each coaching cycle focuses on one to two specific target behaviors;

5. How, and under what conditions, coaching cycles can be discontinued, duplicated or extended based on the progress of each individual teacher.

You've Probably Seen Or Heard This Before

One More Chat With Our Coaches

Rosalina and Jennifer, the coaches we heard from in an earlier chapter, found themselves together at several different times of the day at a training for coaches. Though they had just met, they shared many of the same challenges as relatively new coaches, but their first-year experiences were vastly different. The following transcription is from that same conference where they, and about 80 other instructional coaches from all over the country, were asked to respond in small groups to the following prompt:

> **Do you manage your time as a coach, or is your coaching time managed?**

Rosalina

I definitely manage my time in the sense that I don't really have a fixed schedule other than my small-groups I work with in the afternoon. The teachers know my work schedule – I mean, it's the same as theirs. So they know when I am available. But I have to work hard to schedule coaching sessions and follow-up meetings, and all of that takes way more time than I would have ever thought. A fair amount of my time is spent trying to convince teachers that the coaching can help. I also find that some teachers are not prepared for my coaching sessions, so I show up and we can't really get anything accomplished because they are in the middle of something else. Compared to teaching, I think I have a lot of time that is not scheduled, which is weird, because everything — especially time — seemed so important when I was in the classroom. My coaching job is just different.

Jennifer

Well, our district coaches learned pretty quickly that our time is managed. It's managed by a schedule we have and by the principal at each site; but mainly by the schedule. So, I pretty much have the same Monday schedule, and the same Tuesday schedule, and a schedule for the other days. I mean, my assignments —whether that is in-class coaching, or working with teachers to co-plan out of class — are basically set for each day of the week. The majority of my time is in teachers' classrooms doing coaching. The scheduling of teachers is handled mostly by the principal and follows the time blocks we worked out before school started. Yes, my coaching time is definitely managed.

The Coaching Clock

Time is something that many people can't find enough of, while for others, the clock seems to have stopped as time drags on. In educational organizations, time plays a pivotal role in both the design and operation of the entire enterprise. The number of school days is fixed by time, the duration of the school day is delimited by time, instructional minutes per subject area are sometimes fixed by time, and even teacher development efforts are bounded by time. For many teachers, time just flies by as they hurry to squeeze an ever-burgeoning list of subjects and tasks into an already full day. School and district leaders frequently lament that their time is dominated by meetings, understanding new state and federal initiatives, and the daily dose of crises that seem to demand immediate attention. Against what can be a hectic and eclectic mix of time demands, schools, teachers and leaders are asked to improve themselves. Well-intentioned educators frequently by asking *when* these comprehensive improvement projects are to be designed, implemented and managed. A better question to ask is *how* teachers and educational leaders can better leverage their available time to maximally impact teacher and school improvement.

But for improvement systems to function properly in educational environments requires a set of structures, time allocations and control mechanisms that are frequently lacking. The presence of such systems would better maximize return on investment, both of time, money and human resources. As we saw in the scenario at the start of this chapter, a coaching program can either be the paragon of time-use efficiency or a systematic waste machine for time. The Coaching Clock™ prescribes a structured and logical system for allocating and monitoring a coach's time. For teachers, all guesswork is eliminated as to what the coach does, when it happens, and in what order. For school and district leaders, the coach's time and impact is made evident and accountable. For coaches, the great majority of their time is designed to be spent where it makes the most difference — in classrooms working with teachers. Let's take a look at how The Coaching Clock™ works.

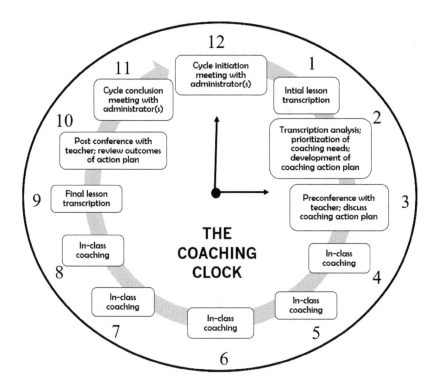

This 12-step system, represented by the hands of a (non-digital) clock, shows each step of a complete coaching cycle. Recall that coaching cycles with a single teacher or a group of teachers can and should repeat endlessly through a year, or indeed, the entire career of a teacher. Where a coach is faced with working with many teachers, it may be the case that most teachers participate in two to three cycles per year. Let's take a closer look at each of the activities that comprise a coaching cycle and how the clock prescriptively guides those.

12:00: Cycle Initiation Meeting

A mixed message to a teacher about their performance from two different sources usually serves to instill mistrust, confusion and sometimes fear. A continual diet of mixed messages can quickly extinguish a motivation to improve. And so it is too with coaching. If the information about coaching – its purpose, its practices, its impact, its structure – is different between a teacher's coach and his or her site leader, the process is off to a bad start and is potentially doomed before rounding the first turn. If such mixed messaging happens regularly, a teacher's frustration can build and fester until the process of coaching is not only seen as ineffective, but unwelcomed. And then they share their experiences and feelings with others. Game over.

To avoid this, the coaching cycle begins and ends with clear communication between the coach and site or district leader. This is not to say that the administrator prescribes what behaviors the coach should target for each individual teacher, but they do have direct impact on that decision. In many cases, a district initiative will dictate the behaviors to be addressed during a coaching cycle. In the case of a district-level coach, this conversation allows the site administrator to inform the coach of specific campus goals that should be the focus of site coaching sessions.

The initial 12 o'clock meeting also allows the coach to identify which teachers are beginning a cycle, or where other teachers are on a cycle. The coach and administrator work together at this point to ensure that only one party is providing feedback to the teacher about instruction. If the coach is working to improve a particular behavior and the principal provides positive feedback — even as a well-intentioned passing comment regarding the target behavior — teachers will often self-certify their expertise and no longer see a benefit in working with the coach. Similarly, if the coach has just provided the teacher evidence of improvement regarding a particular behavior, but the principal leaves feedback citing the targeted behavior as an area in need of refinement, the teacher will often become frustrated and assume that the coaching process has been ineffective. Mixed messages are coaching program killers. Take the time to get this initial activity right.

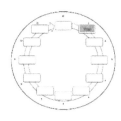

1:00 Initial Lesson Transcription

In a previous chapter we discussed *Data-Driven Observation* as one of the methods of Performance-Based Coaching™. Here is a logical place for the use of that method. For the initial transcription, the coach records the verbal and visual evidence of a teacher's lesson. This creates a written record that can be analyzed with the teacher to describe and discuss current practices. This is also the appropriate time to define terms — remember the acronym *D.I.G.*? The purpose of the transcription is not to evaluate the teacher or to determine if a teacher needs to be coached. Such a use of the data would communicate to all teachers that coaching is only needed for teachers who are not proficient. Instead, the transcription is used specifically as an objective snapshot of what was observed and as a way to set a baseline observation of the behavior or behaviors that will be targeted. This baseline quantitative data will be used again at the end of the coaching cycle to clearly demonstrate evidence of teacher improvement regarding the targeted behavior.

It's also worth noting that the lesson transcription serves a second important purpose, and one that is sometimes not initially recognized. By comparing the initial lesson transcription to an end-of-cycle transcription, we can draw conclusions about the effectiveness of the coach in helping teachers to implement new behaviors and skills. Coaches can use this information to further inform their own self-development plans and efforts.

Here are two examples of lesson transcriptions from the 1:00 o'clock position on the clock.

Sample Reading Lesson Transcript

Teacher's Lesson Objective: We can identify the moral or lesson that the author is trying to teach the audience.

Time	Teacher	Students	Notes
10:00	Who was the main character in our story this week?	The dragon.	Students are sitting on colored squares on the carpet. The teacher has a large reading book on the easel.
	What do we know about him?	He was scared of everything.	She has just finished reading the story to the class as they listened.
10:01	That's right! We know that he was nervous and scared a lot. Wasn't he?	Yes.	
	Do you remember what he was scared of?	Yes.	
	What?	Everything!	
	Like what?	bees the wind spiders his shadow	
10:03	Wow! That is a lot to be scared of. You are all such good readers.		
	Do you remember where the story took place?	The cave	
10:04	Where in the cave? Was it in the cave or near the cave?	Near the cave.	
	What was it like there?	It had flowers and grass and sun and bugs.	
10:06	Yes. Good job. The cave was near a meadow. Do you know what a meadow is?	Yes	

Continued Sample Reading Lesson Transcript

Teacher's Lesson Objective: We can identify the moral or lesson that the author is trying to teach the audience.

Time	Teacher	Students	Notes
	What is it?	It has grass and flowers and bugs.	
10:08	Yes, but what kind of place is it?	(Silence)	
	It is a big open area like a field with no trees. Tell your partner what a meadow is…ready…go!	It is a big area with no trees.	
	Great job. Eyes up here.		
	OK, let me find it…Here it is. What was dragon doing on this page?	He is scared.	
10:10	Yes. He is scared but what is he doing?	He has a shield but it's just a rock.	
	You're right. He is using the rock as a shield to protect him from the birds. See how he is holding it over his head.	Yeah	
10:12	He doesn't want those birds to swoop down and hit him, does he?	No Or bite him Or peck him	.
	No, that wouldn't be good.		
	Did dragon need to be scared of these things?	No	
	So what did we learn from the story?	Don't be scared.	
10:15	Awesome job class. Did you like that story?	Yes	

<u>Sample Math Lesson Transcript</u>

Teacher's Lesson Objective: We can solve two-step algebra problems.

Time	Teacher	Students	Notes
11:15	Solve this problem on your white boards. (x - 3 = 6)		Students are sitting at individual desks.
			Students have whiteboards and dry-erase markers
11:18	Hold up your boards.		
	Good. Good. Good. Check your math. Good. Check yours too.		
11:19	Boards down.		
	How about this problem? (2x – 3 = 6)		
30 sec. passed	Two minutes…		
	One minute…		
	Boards up.		
11:19	OK, let's look at that one.		
11:20	Remember, on this problem we have to what, class?	Find x	
11:22	Yes, but what do we do?	Solve for the variable	
	How do we do that?	Get x by itself.	
	What do we need to do first?	Inverse operations	

<u>Continued Sample Math Lesson Transcript</u>

Teacher's Lesson Objective: We can solve two-step algebra problems.

Time	Teacher	Students	Notes
11:23	Yes. So we are going to add 3 to both sides.		
	If you did that say yessss!	Yesss!	
	Then we need to divide both sides by 2.	Yesss!	
	Now what do we have to remember to do?	Circle the answer.	
	That's right. Circle your answer so I can find it.		
	Hold up your boards in 5...4...3...2...1...boards up.		
11:24	If you have x = 3 you are correct. Who had that the first time?	(10 hands go up)	
	Who knows where they made a mistake?	(Five hands go up)	
	Who knows how to do it now?	(All hands go up)	
11:27	Ok, show me how to do this problem. Ready, go! (3x – 4 = 5)		
	Two minutes...		
	One minute...		
	Boards up.		
11:30	Good. Good. Good Boards down. Much better.		

2:00 Transcription Analysis

Notice that both transcripts only record what is overtly seen or heard in the classroom during the observation. Let's revisit the types of questions that our evidence-gathering is designed to answer during a *Data-Driven Observation.*

- Make sure you are recording only visual and oral information that answers a quantitative question.

- *Data-Driven Observations* answer questions like: How many? How often? or What percentage? These questions tackle total quantity (number of times something was observed) as well as quantity with respect to numbers of opportunities provided (i.e., teacher asked students to answer the same question seven times; students answered three times).

Determine the target behavior that you are going to quantify and implement a simple notation system throughout the transcript that notes the correct use of the behavior as well as missed opportunities for the behavior. This simple notation system can be used to quantify the number of times a targeted behavior was observed as well as the percentage of the observed behavior in relation to the total number of opportunities for the behavior. To find the percentage of time a behavior was utilized properly, use this equation: proper use of behavior divided by total uses of behavior. Thus, 10 /20= 50%.

Don't get bogged down by thinking you have to utilize a particular notation system. As long as it is based on visible and audible information, and it is understandable to you, it will work just fine for the purposes of this time slot.

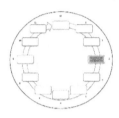

3:00 Pre-Conference with Teacher

Much like the transcript and the analysis, the pre-conference phase of The Coaching Clock™ only addresses what was explicitly seen or heard during the lesson observation.

During the pre-conference, the coach takes on the role of both the reporter and the goal setter. The coach is not an evaluator, as they are not providing feedback regarding the subjective quality of the lesson that was observed. Instead, the coach reports what was observed or heard, where opportunities were correctly executed or missed, and then sets a goal for the subsequent coaching sessions. The coach will also outline the coaching methods that will be used during the cycle, as well as explain how communication between coach and teacher during the lesson will be handled.

Here is a sample pre-conference discussion guide to use during this phase of The Coaching Clock™. At this point, you would only complete the left column items.

Coaching Action Plan

	PRE-CONFERENCE	*POST-CONFERENCE*
Targeted Coaching Objective	*What is the objective of this coaching cycle?*	*At the end of this coaching cycle, was the objective achieved?*
Coaching Method	*Which coaching method(s) will be used to meet the objective above? Why?*	*How was the selected coaching method effective in achieving the objective?*
Physical Reminder of Goal	*What will physically exist in the classroom and/or lesson plan that will remind the teacher to stay focused on his/her teaching objective?*	*How did the physical reminder of his/her coaching objective help him/her to achieve it?*

4:00 – 8:00 In-Class Coaching

Logically, the major allocation of a coach's time is for the use of the methods of Performance-Based Coaching™ previously detailed. This mix of methods is determined by the coach based on the lesson transcription and the teacher's input during the initial conference. It is typical for this part of the clock to run from two to three weeks in duration. Here are three sample "method mixes" based on the established coaching objective.

1. If the teacher has little to no observed implementation of the targeted behavior, the coach might prescribe the following:

Monday	*Structured Lesson Demonstration*
Wednesday	*Co-Plan/Co-Teach*
Thursday	*Pass the Pen*
Monday	*Pass the Pen*
Wednesday	*Real-Time Corrective Feedback*

2. If the teacher demonstrates the targeted behavior, but also missed numerous opportunities for its use, the coach might prescribe the following:

Monday	*Pass the Pen*
Wednesday	*Co-Plan/Co-Teach*
Thursday	*Pass the Pen*
Tuesday	*Real-Time Corrective Feedback*
Friday	*Real-Time Corrective Feedback*

3. If the teacher regularly implements the targeted behavior with only few missed opportunities, the coach might prescribe the following:

Monday	Co-Plan/Co-Teach
Tuesday	Pass the Pen
Thursday	Real-Time Corrective Feedback
Tuesday	Real-Time Corrective Feedback
Friday	Real-Time Corrective Feedback

Notice that each coaching method moves the responsibility of instruction from the coach to the teacher, consistent with our overall goal of moving teachers to independence as discussed in the previous chapter. Remember, every teacher has a different mix of experience, skill and independence, so a *Structured Lesson Demonstration* may not be needed for every lesson in every cycle any more than any other coaching method is needed.

As the coach, you oversee prescribing the particular mix of coaching methods that will be used to accelerate the change in each teacher's behavior. This mix can be adjusted and modified as the cycle progresses, much like an athletic trainer adjusts the mix of exercises based on observed results.

9:00 Final Lesson Transcription

Much like the pre-observation, the final lesson transcription is used as a data point that will determine if the teacher's proper use of the targeted behavior has changed over time. It also provided valuable feedback related to the effectiveness of the coach at changing teacher behaviors.

During the final lesson transcription, the coach again records the observable and audible evidence related to the targeted behavior. This transcript is analyzed only for evidence of the targeted skill, since that has been the focus of the coaching cycle. For some teachers who have worked with a coach for several cycles, the transcription would include information about previously developed behaviors as well.

Based on the level of independence a particular teacher has demonstrated with the targeted behavior, this cycle-concluding transcription should be scheduled strategically. If the teacher remains at a level of *cautious independence* or below on the Continuum of Interdependence™, the post observation should be scheduled during the same subject area or instructional period as the initial lesson observation. This minimizes the number of variables that might impact the teacher's implementation of the targeted behavior, thus providing more reliable information regarding the teacher's progress. If the teacher has reached the stage of *independently confident* or *strategically innovative* along the continuum, then it is important to schedule the final lesson transcription during a different period and subject area. By scheduling this way, the coach is better able to assess if the targeted behaviors have been generalized and are being implemented throughout all instructional periods and subjects.

10:00-Post Conference with Teacher

The post conference is a conversation between the teacher and the coach that concludes with the determination of one of three outcomes.

1. The teacher has not made observable progress regarding the target behavior and will continue with the same objective for another cycle.

2. The teacher has made observable progress regarding the target behavior and will begin a new cycle with a different target behavior.

3. The teacher has made observable progress regarding the target behavior but will not begin a new cycle until a future date.

Regardless of which of the above outcomes is most applicable, the post conference focuses on one key question.

What is the quantifiable evidence of improvement regarding the target behavior?

As previously mentioned, the coach is by definition not an evaluator. Their role is not to comment about the subjective quality of the lesson. Comments like, "You are doing so much better at your questioning," or "It's great to see so many students answering more questions during your lessons" provide little in the way of usable or valid evidence of improvement.

Instead, the coach focuses on the increase, decrease or consistency of use of the target behavior from the initial to the final observation. Comments like, "At the beginning of the cycle, you asked individual students to respond to one question every 10 minutes. Now you are asking the entire class to respond to one question every three minutes," are what the teacher needs to hear. "This change in your behavior has increased the amount of student language production during your lessons and drastically decreased the length of time you speak without checking for understanding." This type of summative feedback provides to the teacher and coach clear evidence of improvement and serves to establish a new baseline for future coaching sessions related to the same or a different targeted behavior.

11:00 Cycle Conclusion Meeting

Each coaching cycle is formally concluded with a meeting between the coach and the appropriate site or district leader. Again, one of the goals is to keep outflowing information about coaching consistent between these two positions. Mixed messages are the organizational enemy of effective coaching programs. During this meeting, three things should be clearly articulated.

Guiding Question	What information needs to be articulated?	What is the desired administrator response?
What objectives were accomplished during the coaching cycle?	How specifically has the targeted behavior improved? What is the evidence of improvement? What should the principal expect to see or hear happening in the classroom upon their next observation?	This information is designed to help administrators focus their positive comments and feedback around the empirical progress that has been made during the coaching cycle. When the objective evidence of improvement provided by the coach is echoed by the subjective evaluation of the principal, teachers are affirmed that their efforts paid off. They also become more motivated for their next cycle.

Guiding Question	What information needs to be articulated?	What is the desired administrator response?
What goals were set that are still in progress?	What specific behaviors are still being targeted? What is the difference between the currently observed behavior and the desired outcome? What, if any, evidence of improvement is available so far?	This information is designed to help administrators temper their positive comments and feedback, since they know the end goal has not yet been achieved. Principals should use comparative adjectives, such as *better* or *more*, that do not imply that the teacher has mastered a skill that may be further targeted by the coach.
What are the future objectives that have not yet been set?	What is the next objective for the behavior that has been targeted? What new behavior needs to be targeted in the next cycle? When will the next cycle initiate?	This information is designed to inform principals about what targeted behaviors are coming up next in future coaching cycles. Principals should use this opportunity to point out the need for improvement and to build urgency and motivation for the next cycle.

Things To Ponder Or Discuss

1. What value does the cycle initiation meeting bring to the coaching cycle?

2. How does the focus on quantitative and observable data impact the coach's ability to provide evidence of improvement?

3. Describe your reaction to such a structured way of allocating time for the use of Performance-Based Coaching™.

4. What impact on an organization does the on-going and never-ending use of coaching cycles produce?

5. Does The Coaching Clock™ and its tight structure have the power to attract more qualified people to become coaches?

The Coaches Corner

Coaches, administrators and others in positions of management or supervision are often told to "sandwich" their feedback as a way to make people feel better about the information provided. Put into words, the formula for *sandwiching* sounds like this: Start with a positive comment, then follow with a truthful comment smoothed over to not sound too negative, and then conclude with another positive comment. For example: "Mr. Clark, you are a brilliant scholar, though your choice of professional attire tugs at the boundaries of what most would consider "tasteful", and I particularly admire your ability to craft witticisms that resonate with your audience."

Sandwiching is an affective response to the provision of accurate data, which sometimes is positive and sometimes not. The theory is that by "hiding" the potentially negative feedback within the two happy pieces of surrounding bread, we somehow effect performance changes without the unseemly practice of using just facts. While this practice seems great in theory as a way of buttressing the morale of the individual, or of a group, it does little to accelerate behavioral change. After all, with this technique everyone gets two out of three correct. By using a positive comment (sometimes an invented one based on no evidence) both at the beginning and end of the feedback, the net effect is to change the entire tonality and function of the communication from one that creates urgency for change to one that is more a suggestion that may or may not be followed.

Listen to the difference between these two statements by a doctor after one of the author's annual physical.

Version A – "Mr. Williams, your blood pressure is fifteen points higher than your last visit. You need to see a nutritionist and begin exercising more regularly to get these numbers under control."

Version B – "Mr. Williams, your blood work came back and there is no sign of cancer or other illness. Your blood pressure is fifteen points higher than your last visit. You need to see a nutritionist and begin exercising more regularly, but overall we don't need to put you on any medication at this time so that's a good thing."

My relationship with the doctor isn't damaged by the first statement. In fact, after following his advice and improving my blood pressure, we both reap the benefit. Further, I am not offended nor do I like my doctor less because of his data-based, non-sandwiched information. His job is to maximize my health; it is not to make me feel good about being unhealthy even though he likes my new shoes.

The Leaders Lounge

Be honest.

Question 1

How many times have you been a party to a mixed message that stifled improvements at your site or with a specific teacher?

Question 2

How hard do you work daily to minimize – if not eliminate – mixed messages that can put an arrow through you and your teachers' efforts to improve instruction?

Question 3

Have you ever *not* confronted someone who you knew was deliberately inventing or spreading mixed messages that were harmful to your organization?

These are hard questions, but they demand answers. The weather cannot be cold and hot at the same time, and we would never venture to let people hear such nonsense. On a more personal level, we fight doggedly for our children and other close relationships to ensure that our messages are singular and clear. Instructional coaching can die a quick death if you allow, engage in, or ignore mixed messages. Go get 'em!

Fun Quiz

1. The purpose of the cycle initiation meeting is for the principal to choose what teacher skills the coach will target during the cycle.
   a. true
   b. false
   c. not sure

2. The teacher is responsible for setting their own goals for each coaching cycle.
   a. true
   b. false
   c. not sure

3. The teacher should _____ choose what coaching methods the coach implements during a coaching cycle.
   a. always
   b. sometimes
   c. never

4. It is the coach's responsibility to inform the site administrator regarding the outcomes of each coaching cycle.
   a. true
   b. false
   c. not sure

5. Part of a coach's performance review should include information related to the quantitative improvement of teacher skills across coaching cycles.
   a. always
   b. sometimes
   c. never

Chapter 12
Conclusion

The Time is Now

We wrote this book because of a glaring implementation gap in public education between what teachers know and what they actually do while planning for and delivering instruction. Even 15 years ago, our discussions with school and district leaders about this phenomenon were held behind closed doors and were frequently uncomfortable. For their part, leaders frequently and in good faith responded in a familiar fashion: "But we sent everybody to the training." More accurately, several of these leaders had already identified the real truth: "We have sent many teachers to many trainings for many years and expected them to implement those many things." In the great majority of cases, schools and districts described professional development efforts that followed essentially the same formula:

1. Identify a need, respond to a mandate, chase the latest shiny object
2. Send teachers to training
3. Buy materials to support the effort
4. Hope, wish, beg, mandate teachers to implement what they learned
5. Repeat cycle

The paradox of the implementation gap is that well-intentioned school and district leaders have worked hard to bring to their teachers the latest in educational innovations. Sadly, those innovations are largely un-implemented. Educational leaders, policy makers and the general populace have erroneously assumed that more innovation will bring more implementation. Clarifying terms might help. Innovation is about new ideas, new information, or new processes that create opportunities for growth and development for both users and end-users (read: teachers and students). At an organizational level, innovation should result in the abandonment of old belief systems and practices in order to adopt new and better things that bring about significant advances. But an unimplemented innovation is the same as no innovation at all.

Somewhat different from other professions, teachers are provided a steady menu — mandated in most states — of learning opportunities. Presumably, what they learn could help students to learn better, teachers to teach better, and schools and districts to perform better for more students. But the chase for bringing innovation to educators seems to have overshadowed what should be an equally furtive and purposeful chase for ways to bridge the implementation gap; to help teachers put what they know into action — quickly. In private industry, an implementation gap can mean the end of the business. If people prefer to wait less than four seconds for a web page to load, and your company's web page loads in six seconds, you may lose customers. If your web page loads slowly because your web design company failed to implement new information that makes page loading faster, that company may be shuttered tomorrow. Increasingly, organizations seeking to stay relevant read up and hire experts to help them with a new field known as "knowledge translation". Getting new knowledge put into immediate use by employees to improve products and processes in as short a time as possible is what this new field of KT is all about.

The benefits of shortened or eliminated implementation gaps are all around us. The speed of innovation and application has changed most of our lives in areas ranging from health care to cell phones to pet care to how we use maps. Magnetic resonance imaging (MRI) machines that were as big as semi-trucks 10 years ago are now the size of a refrigerator; a phone or computer made in June of this year is likely to have five additional features compared to the same one made in January of the same year. The examples are endless and they all point to successful processes and practices for getting people to use what they know. When we talk of implementation gaps, we are unfortunately referring to an organizational failure to gain people's skilled, consistent and committed use of an innovation. When we can speak of the same gap in an organization year after year, then we have to conclude that the process or system of educating its people is not working. It is in what organizational experts call the "last mile" of its utility. We have argued in this book that traditional development efforts for teachers have reached the end of their usefulness. A new view is needed.

Where to Go From Here

As we have detailed in this book, the theory and application of Performance-Based Coaching™ has shown great promise for transforming teacher learning, student achievement, and school performance. But coaching is no panacea and half-hearted efforts to implement it usually result in damage that can endure for years.

Coaching as a reactive measure – a quick response to cure a negative situation — is like waiting to see a dentist until your teeth begin to hurt. Sure, the dentist can fill the cavities and fix the accumulated problems, but the process is often costly and painful. Together with oral hygiene, getting regular cleanings that keep your mouth healthy result in fewer issues over time and are much less painful. Comparing anything with going to the dentist is probably a poor analogy, but with both there could be some initial pain before the radiant shine of beautiful teeth. Here are three final thoughts as you consider initiating or expanding coaching for your organization.

1.   Coaching does not replace quality teacher training.

Performance-Based Coaching™ is content neutral; it instead is a unified system of theory and tools to implement what you want teachers to implement. Thus, what you have learned in this book can work with mathematics, language arts or woodshop teachers. What needs to come first is quality training, ideally in methods that help teachers to instruct better. Vacuous theories and ivory-tower musings are difficult to translate into behaviors, and helping teachers to master new behaviors is your professional coach's bread and butter.

2.   Coaching is a big part — usually the highest-leverage part — of a comprehensive system of human and organizational change.

As we have discussed, coaches do not work in isolation. They are maximally effective when they are a part of a comprehensive development structure which includes leadership, clear organizational goals and a commitment to the sometimes-messy process of human development. Coaching accelerates the implementation of innovation, and when the other learning system elements are present and humming, teacher improvement takes off at warp speed.

3. Coaching makes sense mathematically and yields more than a dollar for each dollar invested.

Costs, cost containment, and cost justifications are increasingly visible and important aspects of teacher development. Dollars come from various sources, including those ear-marked for professional development, grant sources, title funds and other local and district sources. We have worked with coaching programs funded almost entirely by private donations. Here is the math to see how far-reaching a single coach's time can go and why an effective coach's value always exceeds their cost to the organization.

One full-time coach with a staff of 20 teachers
- Coach dedicates five hours per day to teacher coaching
- Total coaching time per week: 25 hours
- Total coaching time per month: 100 hours

If that coach were to complete one coaching cycle per month that includes five teachers, each teacher would receive 20 hours of in-class coaching on behaviors related to school or district initiatives.

Over the course of an academic year, here are the figures:
- Total in-class coaching time in a year: 1,000 hours
- Total teachers coached: 20, with each doing 2.5 complete coaching cycles per year
- Amount of coaching time per teacher: 50 hours

As can be seen from these figures, a re-framing of how professional development dollars are spent, and how coaching time is allocated, can bring about new ways of looking at the system-wide impact of effective coaching. Let's go back to the dentist: would you rather have one big visit to the dentist every couple of years that costs a ton of money and only fixes your accumulated problems? Or does daily hygiene, regular visits to the dentist, a lower price tag and improved dental health sound better?

A New And Exciting View

The morphing landscape of student preparation and performance has brought extreme focus to the area of teacher development. As we discussed at the outset of this book, more and more parents, politicians and educators are questioning the traditional methods of teacher education. Board members, citizens and policy makers are asking to see results in exchange for funding. At a time when businesses, healthcare and social service providers are shortening their implementation timelines, education seems in many cases to be extending theirs. But there is hope.

Performance-Based Coaching™ gains traction with educators because, among other things, it rejects the idea that teacher learning happens only at two or three fixed points during the year and in a location away from students and the dynamics of real classrooms. Industry and business recognized more than 50 years ago that what is needed is a continuous improvement process, characterized by prescriptive and predictive models of learning that foster and support efficiency, excellence and sustainability. Effective practices must be retained, but inefficient and parochial methods and behaviors that are comfortable — but not working — simply must go. Teacher learning can move from a private act to one that is characterized by meaningful collaboration with experts working toward measurable objectives in real time. Among the many winners from this new view of teacher learning are those for whom the enterprise is designed and operated: students.

The time is now.

Sources

Chapter 2

1. Deutschman, Alan. *Change or Die.* New York, NY: HarperCollins Publishers, 2007.
2. Ibid.

Chapter 4

1. Deming, W. Edwards. *The New Economics for Industry, Government, and Education.* Boston, MA: MIT Press. *1993.*
2. Senge, Peter M. *The Fifth Discipline Fieldbook: Strategies and Tools for Building a Learning Organization.* New York: Currency, Doubleday, 1994.
3. Costa, A.L. & Garmston, R.J. *Cognitive coaching: A foundation for renaissance schools.* Norwood, MA: Christopher-Gordon Publishers, Inc. 1994.
4. Retrieved from www.cognitivecoachingtraining.com on June 2, 2018
5. Ibid.
6. Flaherty, J. *Coaching: Evoking excellence in others.* Boston, MA: Butterworth-Heinemann. 1999.
7. Willerman, McNeely and Koffman. *Teachers Helping Teachers: Peer Observation and Assistance.* New York, NY: Praeger. 1991.
8. Festinger, L. *A theory of cognitive dissonance.* Evanston, Ill. Row, Peterson. 1957

CPSIA information can be obtained
at www.ICGtesting.com
Printed in the USA
FFHW02n2139161018
48826561-52999FF